FOS

6/11

express housekeeping

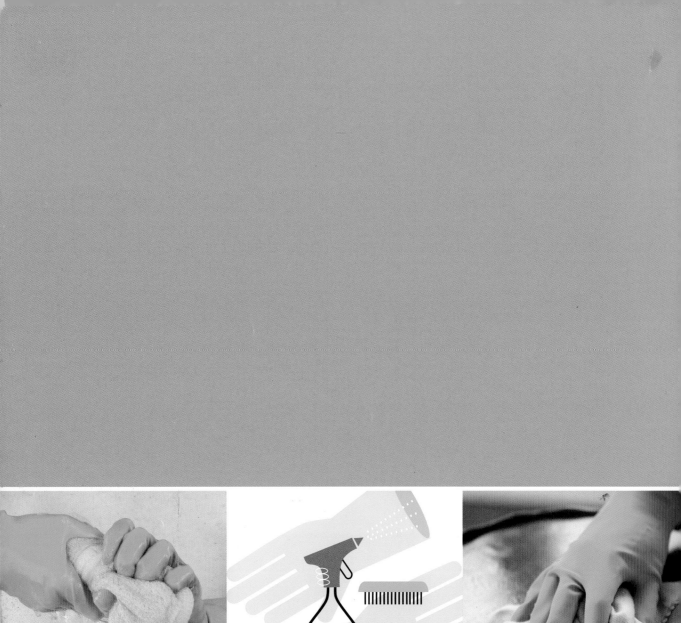

express
housekeeping

How to speed clean Lighten the laundry load Cleaning tricks & tips

Anna Shepard

Editor Hilary Mandleberg
Art Editor Miranda Harvey
Photographer Howard Shooter
Illustrator Sean Sims @ New Division

DK UK
Senior Editor Scarlett O'Hara
Senior Art Editor Jane Ewart
Editorial Assistant Kajal Mistry
US Editor Margaret Parrish
Managing Editor Dawn Henderson
Managing Art Editor Marianne Markham
Senior Jacket Creative Nicola Powling
Senior Presentations Creative
Caroline de Souza
Senior Production Editor Jennifer Murray
Senior Production Controller Alice Sykes
Creative Technical Support Sonia Charbonnier

First published in the United States in 2011
by DK Publishing
375 Hudson Street, New York, New York 10014

11 12 13 14 15 10 9 8 7 6 5 4 3 2 1
179888—Mar/2011
A catalog record for this book
is available from the Library of Congress.
ISBN 978-0-7566-7177-8

Printed and bound in Singapore by
Tien Wah Press

Discover more at **www.dk.com**

Contents

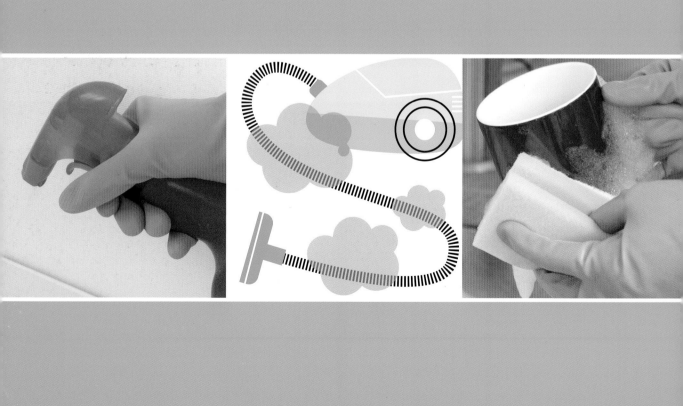

Introduction

At last! Now there's no need to spend half your life cleaning your home. With the expert tips, tricks, and time-saving strategies in this book, you can get it all done with maximum speed and efficiency—most of the tasks in the following pages take less than 10 minutes to do (excluding soaking, standing, and drying times).

Cleaning little and often is the smart, pain-free way to keep the dust and dirt under control—that, plus regular decluttering. There's no greater time-waster than sorting and tidying before you can even reach for the vacuum cleaner, so keep your house in order and you're halfway to keeping it clean.

And you don't need a huge supply of cleaning equipment and chemical cleaners. Your pantry contains items that clean just as well as branded products—and they offer an appealingly greener and thriftier alternative.

If you're juggling a full, busy life with running a home, this book will be a life-saver. You'll get the house sparkling clean, superfast—so you can get on with the rest of your life!

Basic kit

It's impossible to create one cleaning kit that suits every scenario, but here are the basics. Invest in a plastic tote to carry your kit around the house with you as you work. You're more likely to keep the dirt under control if you can grab the product you need quickly. The key to keeping your home clean with minimum effort is to tackle jobs promptly and do little and often.

BLEACH
Use to disinfect and prevent mold and mildew.

DISINFECTANT SPRAY
Use for bathrooms or kitchen counters.

PLASTIC TOTE
Useful for carrying your cleaning kit around the house with you as you work.

DUST CLOTHS
Use these for buffing up a surface after polishing. The green alternative is a piece of old T-shirt.

MICROFIBER CLOTHS
Use these dry or slightly damp for almost any job where you need a cloth.

SCOURERS
Use for scrubbing pans. Buy plastic ones for nonstick pans.

CREAM CLEANER
Good for quickly removing marks from many surfaces.

FLOOR CLEANER
Choose a type that suits your flooring.

SPRAY BOTTLES
Use for environmentally friendly homemade cleaning solutions.

RUBBER GLOVES
Wear for most cleaning jobs to protect your hands.

MEASURING CUP
Useful for mixing small amounts of cleaning solutions.

Storage-closet kit

You'll probably need a storage closet for larger cleaning items. Here are the essentials to help you get your home cleaned to perfection. Keep the things you use most often, such as the dustpan and brush and the vacuum cleaner, near the front of the closet for quick access.

VACUUM CLEANER
Probably the most useful appliance in your cleaning toolkit. Choose one with at least 2 or 3 attachments.

BROOM
Use when you need to sweep messes up quickly instead of getting out the vacuum cleaner.

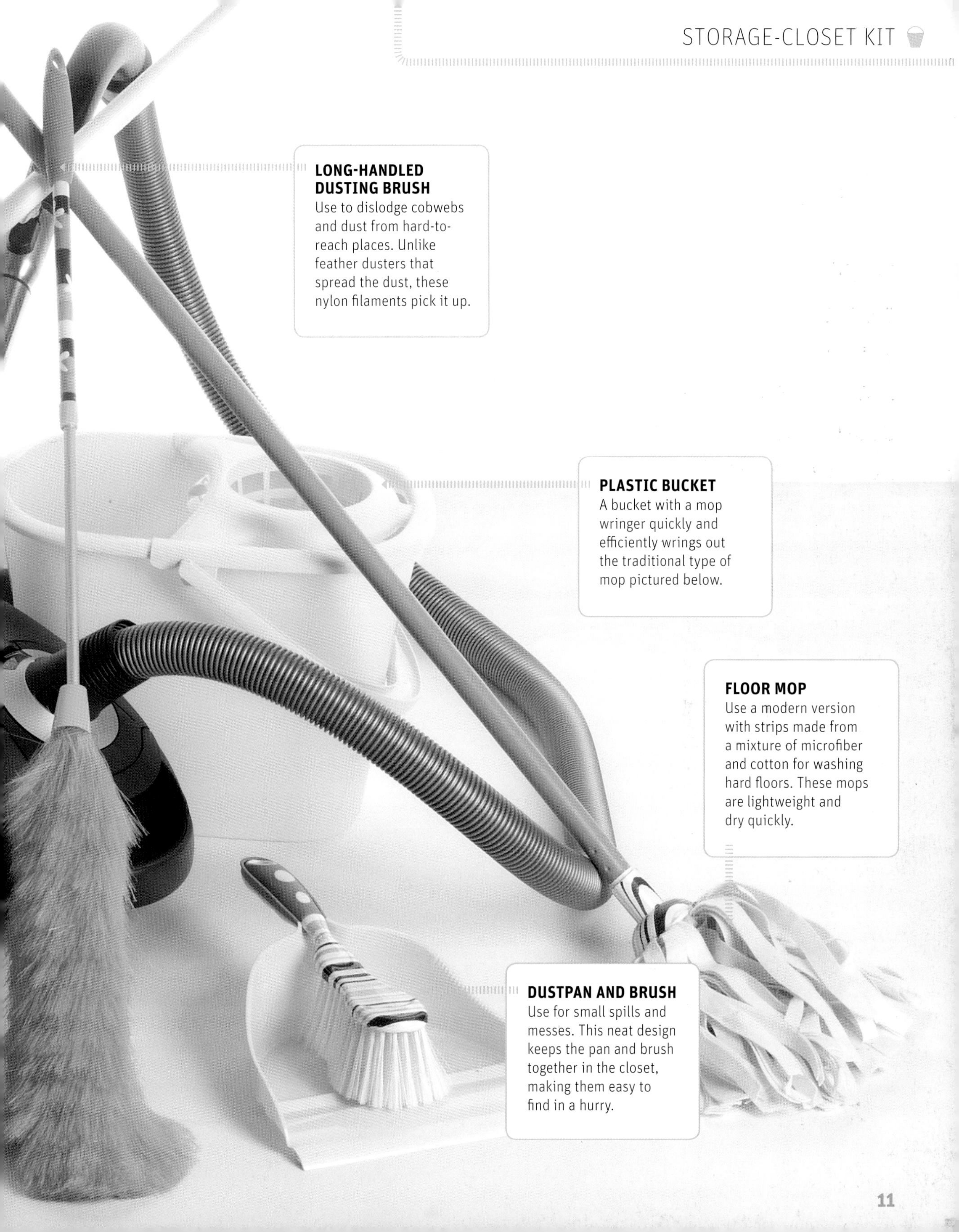

LONG-HANDLED DUSTING BRUSH
Use to dislodge cobwebs and dust from hard-to-reach places. Unlike feather dusters that spread the dust, these nylon filaments pick it up.

PLASTIC BUCKET
A bucket with a mop wringer quickly and efficiently wrings out the traditional type of mop pictured below.

FLOOR MOP
Use a modern version with strips made from a mixture of microfiber and cotton for washing hard floors. These mops are lightweight and dry quickly.

DUSTPAN AND BRUSH
Use for small spills and messes. This neat design keeps the pan and brush together in the closet, making them easy to find in a hurry.

Natural cleaning kit

It's hard to believe that some of the best household cleaners are natural ingredients, but once you've tried vinegar on windows or baking soda on stained mugs, you'll quickly realize their value. Many of these items may already be in your kitchen cupboard. If not, you'll find everything you need in a supermarket, drug store, or hardware store. Make sure you equip yourself with a few spray bottles, too, for applying your homemade cleaning solutions.

SOFT CLOTHS
Use soft knitted cloths made from natural cotton to buff items to a shine.

BAKING SODA
A gentle alternative to using abrasive cleaning products.

BORAX
Good for bleaching whites and deodorizing.

VINEGAR SOLUTION
Made from water and white vinegar, spray wherever you want to break down limescale.

LEMON JUICE
The acid in lemon juice helps dissolve limescale and, combined with salt, it can remove stains.

TEA TREE OIL
A natural disinfectant, it works particularly well on mold and mildew.

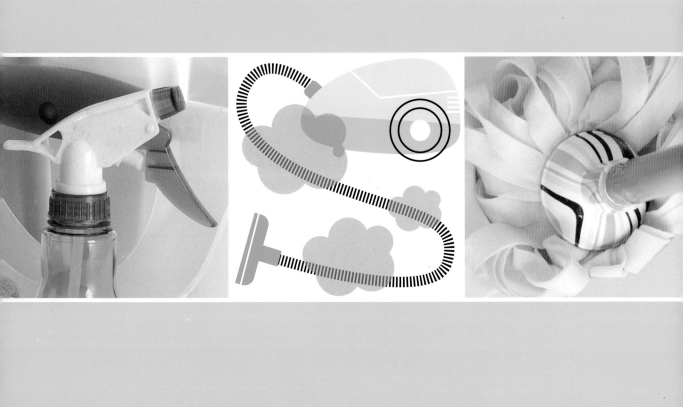

Speed Cleaning

10 MIN Emergency clean up

If your house is in chaos and you have limited time before visitors arrive, don't worry. It's amazing how much you can get done in just 10 minutes—especially once you're armed with our useful checklist of tasks.

1 BE SELECTIVE
Don't try to clean the whole house. Just think about the main area(s) you want to look clean. They're likely to be the kitchen and living room, and you'll probably want to include a whizz around the bathroom.

2 DISPOSE OF GARBAGE
To eliminate bad smells, make sure you dispose of full bags of garbage. Then open the windows to let the fresh air in and perhaps light a few fragranced candles.

3 CLEAR THE TABLES
When tables are cleared and clean, everything will look much better. If there's any paperwork lying around and adding to the clutter, pile it into a box file or folder.

4 CLEAR THE KITCHEN SINK
This might involve doing a few dishes, putting away any dry dishes, and/or loading the dishwasher.

5 PICK UP THE LIVING ROOM
Clear the coffee table and put books and magazines away. Then pile everything else that's cluttering the living room into a basket and tuck it in a corner to sort out later.

6 DEAL WITH CHAIRS AND SOFAS
Check chairs and sofas for crumbs, then plump the pillows and neatly fold any throws over the arms or backs of chairs and sofas.

7 STRAIGHTEN THE RUGS
You won't have time to shake rugs out, but just straightening them and picking up any crumbs and other debris makes all the difference.

8 WHIZZ AROUND THE BATHROOM
Don't get caught up in extensive cleaning. Just wipe around the sink and behind the faucets, check that the toilet's clean, and put away cosmetics.

9 BLITZ THE HALL
Hang up coats and items of clothing. Pile shoes, hats, and other clutter into a hallway basket—keep one in the hall for this purpose.

10 HIDE THE REST
Hide rooms you haven't straightened up by shutting the doors, then adjust the lighting in the rest of the house so dirty corners can't be seen.

Dust surfaces

Dust little but often to keep household dust at bay. Most modern surfaces are designed for easy cleaning—all they require is a quick damp-dust. Dry-dusting takes a little longer, but you need only to dry-dust nonwashable wall surfaces and furniture made from solid wood. Always vacuum after dusting to collect the dust that's settled.

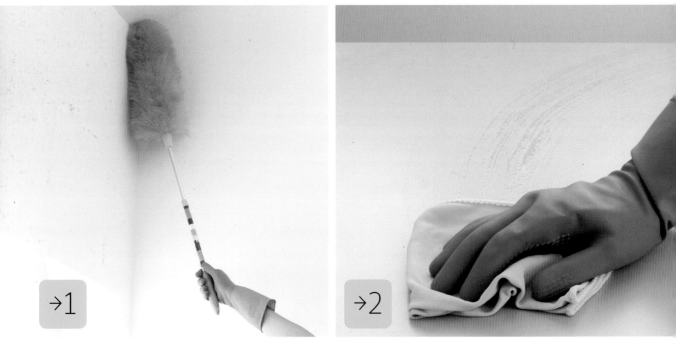

→1

Dust the walls and ceiling, including the corners. Use an extendable brush with nylon filaments. These pick up the dust instead of spreading it around like a feather duster.

→2

Use a damp microfiber cloth to dust any washable surfaces. Be sure to collect the dust by folding it into the cloth and getting rid of it, rather than simply moving it around.

WHAT TO DO WHEN

DAILY → To keep on top of your dusting, get into the habit of dusting something every day, even if it's just a table.

WEEKLY → Dust coffee tables, lampshades (see box opposite), and electronic equipment (use an antistatic cloth for this).

MONTHLY → Dust walls and ceilings, baseboards, and bookshelves.

Dusting a lampshade

First, unplug the lamp, and leave the bulb to cool. Holding the lampshade steady, dust it gently using the dusting-brush attachment and your vacuum cleaner. Work the brush into any gathers or creases. Do not bend the lampshade out of shape. Gently dry-dust the bulb then wipe the base.

→3

Use a clean dust cloth or a dry microfiber cloth to dry-dust nonwashable surfaces. As you work, use oval motions. You are aiming to gather the dust beneath the dust cloth.

→4

Fold the dust cloth to trap the dust, then repeat step 3 with the folded dust cloth. When the dust cloth is too small to continue, shake it out carefully into the garbage, and start again.

Vacuum kit

Investing in a good vacuum cleaner is a major step forward in the battle for a clean home. The main choice is between an upright model, which is good if you have large areas of floor to clean, and a cylinder model, which is best if you have to cope with a lot of stairs. Choose a vacuum with a variety of attachments, then you'll be able to tackle a surprising number of jobs around the home very speedily. Many vacuum cleaners incorporate built-in storage for the smaller attachments.

UPHOLSTERY NOZZLE
Use to vacuum sofas, pillows, curtains, mattresses, and similar furnishings.

CREVICE NOZZLE
Vital for getting into corners and crevices.

ALL-PURPOSE FLOORHEAD
Vacuum carpets by retracting the brushes and hard floors by extending them.

DUSTING BRUSH
Useful for dusting hard surfaces.

TELESCOPIC TUBE
Adjust the length of the tube so you can vacuum without stooping.

HOSE
Today's vacuums have non-kink hoses so the suction power isn't impeded. Choose a model that allows you to adjust the suction— gentler for rugs and curtains, and more powerful for floors.

VACUUM CLEANER
If you opt for a cylinder model, make sure you can comfortably carry it around the house.

FILTER
If you have allergies or pets, choose a vacuum with a High-Efficiency Particulate Air (HEPA) filter that traps the finest particles.

VACUUM CLEANER BAG
Vacuum cleaner bags are easy to dispose of but you need to keep spares.

5 MIN Vacuum a carpeted floor

Vacuum your carpets frequently to help lengthen their life. With today's efficient vacuum cleaners, the job only takes a few minutes and there's no need to move the furniture every time.

BARE ESSENTIALS

vacuum cleaner

carpet floorhead

crevice nozzle

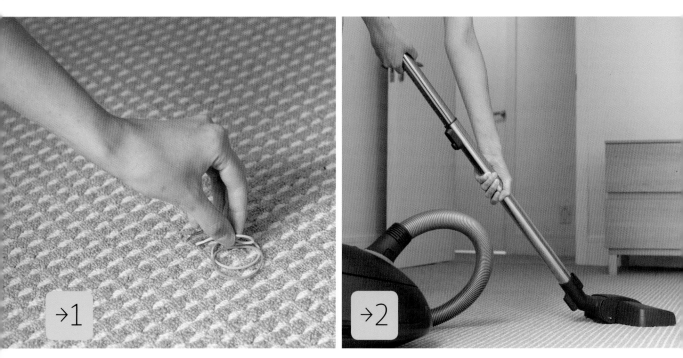

→1

→2

Before you vacuum, pick up any stray pieces of paper, food, or other debris from the carpet that might get sucked into your vacuum cleaner and block it.

Use the carpet floorhead or adjust your upright vacuum cleaner for use on carpets. Starting at the far side of the room, vacuum back and forth, using overlapping strokes.

WHAT TO DO WHEN

EVERY FEW DAYS → Vacuum areas of carpet that get a lot of use. Ground-in dirt will shorten the life of the carpet.

EVERY FEW WEEKS → Pull out beds, tables, and chairs, and vacuum the carpet beneath.

EVERY 2–3 YEARS → Have your carpets professionally cleaned. If there are children or pets in the house, do this every year.

Extra tips

There's no need to set the vacuum cleaner to maximum suction when you're cleaning wall-to-wall carpeting. This will make the job harder and will weaken the fibers of the carpet. Instead, set the vacuum to medium suction and don't press down too hard, but let the vacuum cleaner do the work.

→3

Work toward the door, still making repeated, overlapping strokes. Go over dirty patches several times, since the vacuum will pick up more dust each time.

→4

When you have finished vacuuming the main area of the carpet, attach a crevice nozzle and use this to clean along the baseboards and in the corners.

5 MIN Vacuum carpeted stairs

You don't have to vacuum stairs more than once a week. The key to doing it speedily lies in the preparation. Clear debris and clutter before you begin, then the job will take only a few minutes.

BARE ESSENTIALS

vacuum cleaner

crevice nozzle

carpet floorhead

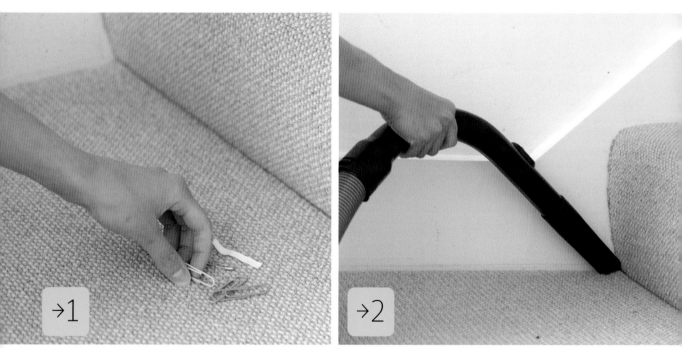

Start by collecting any debris on the stairs that is big enough to clog your vacuum cleaner. Look for things like coins, paper clips, and scraps of paper.

Attach the crevice nozzle to the vacuum cleaner and use it to clean thoroughly in all the corners, where the treads meet the risers, and along the baseboards.

Extra tips

Stairs are often used as dumping grounds for things that are either on their way up or down. For speed and safety as you work, remove any clutter before you begin.

To save time, plug the vacuum cleaner in at a socket that's located conveniently so that you can vacuum as many stairs as possible before you have to unplug it and plug it in again somewhere else.

If you are using a cylinder cleaner, you will have to perch it on a stair and move it as you go. Starting from the bottom and working upward means there's no risk of the machine falling on you as you work.

→3

→4

Using the carpet floorhead or adjusting your upright cleaner for use on carpets, start vacuuming on the bottom step. Vacuum the tread—the horizontal part of the stair.

Swivel the floorhead so you can run it along the riser—the vertical part of the stair. Repeat on each stair, continuing until you reach the top.

Maintain a vacuum cleaner

Modern vacuum cleaners are quick and easy to maintain and should give years of useful service. It's worth spending a few minutes changing the bag and checking the filter regularly to keep it working efficiently.

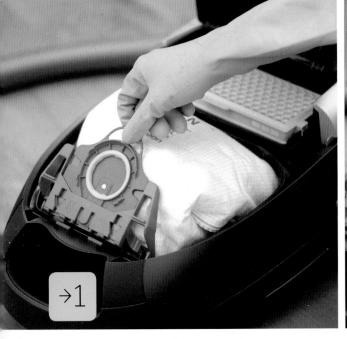

→1

→2

Change the vacuum cleaner bag when it's full. Always do this job outside or in a well-ventilated area, following the manufacturer's instructions.

Check the filter regularly and replace when necessary, following the manufacturer's instructions. Make sure that it stays free of debris so it works efficiently.

Extra tips

Although they don't have a bag, today's bagless vacuums need emptying, too. Empty the dirt container when it's three-quarters full, and occasionally rinse it out and leave it to dry. You also need to clean the filter. It's recommended that you do this every time you empty the dirt container. Follow the manufacturer's instructions.

Look after the exterior of your vacuum cleaner, too. From time to time, unplug it and wipe the wheels with a damp cloth. This removes dirt, which marks carpets, and grit, which damages wooden floors. If you use the vacuum outside to clean the interior of your car, stand it on a rubber mat to stop the wheels from picking up dirt and grit.

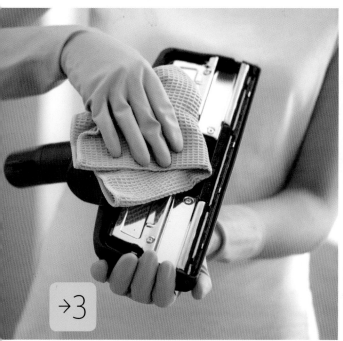

→3

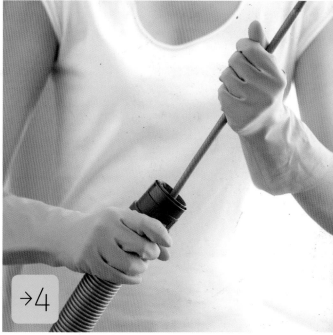

→4

Check the floorhead once a month.
Remove any bits of string or hair that have collected on the brush, then wipe it with a damp microfiber cloth.

If your vacuum stops sucking efficiently, the hose may be blocked. To remove the blockage, gently push a bamboo stick down the hose. Don't use force or you could damage the machine.

10 MIN Clean curtains

Cleaning curtains is easily overlooked but doing it will help prolong their life. It's a quick and easy job and you only need to do it once a year. In between, simply vacuum them from time to time.

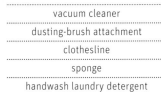

BARE ESSENTIALS

vacuum cleaner

dusting-brush attachment

clothesline

sponge

handwash laundry detergent

→1

Close the curtains then vacuum them, moving from top to bottom along the entire width of the curtain. Use the dusting-brush attachment and minimum suction.

→2

Turn the curtain back to vacuum the wrong side. Again, vacuum from top to bottom. Take care to clean this side thoroughly, since it often gathers the most dirt.

Cleaning Roman blinds

A Roman blind made from a fabric that is washable can be laundered, but it will involve unstitching the blind and sewing it back together afterward. A speedier alternative is to use a foam upholstery cleaning product. Try it out first on an inconspicuous area of the blind to make sure that the color in the fabric doesn't run. After you've applied the cleaner, wipe it off carefully using a dry cloth. If upholstery cleaner doesn't work, you'll have to call in a specialized cleaner.

Prevention is better than cure, so vacuum Roman blinds regularly with the dusting-brush attachment. You can also have the blind treated with a stain-resistant finish.

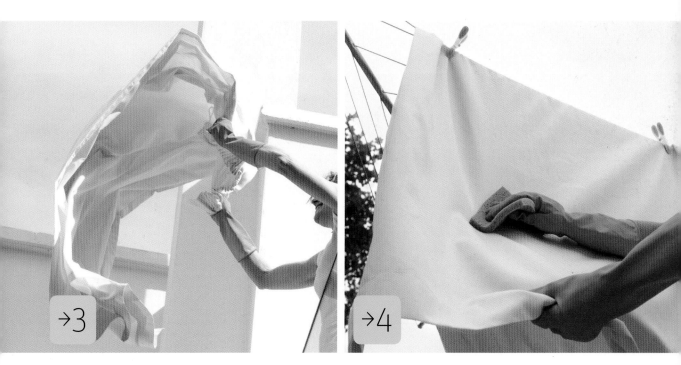

→3

Take the curtains down and shake them well outdoors to remove any dust you may have missed. Hang over the clothesline to air—preferably outside—for several hours.

→4

With the curtains on the line, check for stains. Remove them, using a barely damp sponge and a little handwash laundry detergent. When the curtains are dry, rehang.

10 TIPS Rug and carpet care

The shoes-off rule is the answer to many people's effort to keep carpets clean. Others prefer to make fewer demands of guests and put up with the consequences. Either way, you'll need to vacuum rugs and carpets regularly and check for stains.

1 USE GOOD UNDERLAY
When laying new carpet, choose good-quality underlay for extra cushioning. It also helps prevent dirt from being ground into the carpet and makes it easier to be collected by the vacuum.

2 FLATTEN CURLING EDGES
If the edge of a carpet or rug starts to roll up, press it flat or someone might trip. Lay a damp pressing cloth (a square of linen or cotton cloth will do) on the edge and iron it firmly using a medium setting.

3 USE A DOORMAT
Use doormats at each entrance to your home, ideally inside and outside. This makes a big difference in preventing rugs and carpet from gathering dirt.

4 KEEP THE CURTAINS DRAWN
If light is making a favorite rug or carpet fade, try to keep the curtains drawn at sunny times, especially if the room isn't in use.

5 LIFT THE FURNITURE
Always lift furniture when you move it around a room. Never push or drag it across the carpet, since this will damage the pile.

6 REPOSITION RUGS
Turn rugs around regularly or change their position to even out wear and avoid damage done by furniture. It will also help to even out fading caused by sunlight (see tip 4).

7 BEAT OUT THE DUST
A couple of times a year, ideally on a bright, windy day, take rugs outside, fling them over the clothesline, and beat them with a broom or tennis racket. Seek professional advice for a valuable rug.

8 VACUUM REGULARLY
This is your first line of defense. Vacuum rugs and carpets every week. Dirt and dust make rugs and carpets look grubby, and they hasten the appearance of worn patches.

9 AVOID WASHING RUGS
Unless otherwise advised by the care label, the general rule is that it's best not to wash rugs. Instead, deal with individual stains with warm water and carpet detergent.

10 AVOID OVERCLEANING
Professional carpet cleaning ages carpets so try to keep from getting them dirty in the first place. As long as you vacuum regularly, you can get away with professional cleaning just once every 3 years.

10 MIN Clean a venetian blind

Blinds look tricky to clean but they don't have to take long. And you don't need special equipment—just a vacuum cleaner and a damp cloth. Do this quick clean with the blind still hanging at the window.

BARE ESSENTIALS

vacuum cleaner with dusting-brush attachment

microfiber cloth

all-purpose cleaning spray

→1

Lower the blind fully and close the slats. Keeping the blind steady, gently dust the closed slats using the dusting-brush attachment on your vacuum cleaner.

→2

Now open the slats of the blind and vacuum them again. This time, make sure that you get the brush into as many nooks and crannies as possible.

Quick cleans for other blinds

Vacuum vertical blinds using the dusting-brush attachment or a special blind-cleaning tool.

Clean nonwashable roller blinds by vacuuming with the dusting-brush attachment. From time to time, take the blind down, lay it on a clean flat surface, and vacuum the back.

Clean washable roller blinds with a well-wrung-out sponge and upholstery shampoo. Rinse each side by sponging with clean water, and drying with an old towel. Rehang it while it's still a little damp.

Vacuum wooden venetian blinds with the dusting-brush attachment or use a dry sock worn on your hand. Do not use water.

→3

→4

With the slats still open, wipe the blinds with a damp microfiber cloth or with a dampened sock worn on your hand. Make sure you don't bend the slats as you work.

Close the slats and if there are still any marks, squirt them with an all-purpose cleaning spray. Finish by wiping with a damp microfiber cloth.

10 MIN Quick window clean

When you don't have time to clean windows thoroughly, you can easily get away with a quick wipe and polish. Just focus on the dirty spots, and leave the major cleaning for once or twice a year.

BARE ESSENTIALS

measuring cup

spray bottle

white vinegar

sponge

microfiber cloth

→1

→2

Make a mixture of 1 part white vinegar to 4 parts water and use this to fill a plastic spray bottle. This homemade window-cleaner works as well as bought products.

Before you spray the window, wet a sponge, squeeze it out, and use it to remove the worst of the fingerprints, smudges, and other dirty marks on the glass.

ACTION PLAN

BEFORE YOU START → Move furniture out of the way for easy access to the window.

AS YOU WORK → Spray the vinegar and water mixture sparingly or it will involve more work to buff and dry.

AFTERWARD → Rinse the vinegar from your sponge before you put it away.

Quick mirror clean

Quickly buff a mirror to a shine using a microfiber cloth squeezed out in water. If the mirror's very grubby, squeeze a sponge out in warm water mixed with a little dishwashing liquid. Wipe the mirror with the damp sponge, then buff it with a dry microfiber cloth.

→3

→4

With a clean, squeezed-out sponge at the ready, spray the vinegar solution on the window, one area at a time. Use the sponge to rub the solution in.

Still concentrating on one area of the window at a time and working quickly to prevent streaking, buff the glass dry using a dry microfiber cloth.

25 MIN Thorough window clean

Once or twice a year, clean your windows thoroughly, including the frames, to remove any dust and mildew. It won't take long, and windows and frames will stay clean for several months.

BARE ESSENTIALS

microfiber cloths

wash tub

bleach, knitted cloth

bucket

white vinegar, sponge

→1

→2

Start by dusting the frame with a dry microfiber cloth to remove any cobwebs. Make sure you dust every surface of the frame, both vertical and horizontal.

Wipe the frame with a soft damp cloth, then, to eliminate mildew, make a solution of 1 part bleach with 3 parts water. Wring the cloth out in this, then wipe again.

BEFORE YOU BEGIN

ARRANGE A TOWEL → Lay a towel on the sill or on the floor, to collect any water drips.

MOVE FURNITURE → Get all furniture out of the way so you have safe and easy access to the windows.

SET UP A STEP LADDER → Essential for high windows. Make sure it's securely erected.

Extra tips

Stubborn marks on windows can be removed with undiluted methylated spirits. Apply it directly to the mark on one cloth, then rinse with a clean cloth squeezed out in water.

Polish and dry in step 4 using scrunched-up newspaper. This old-fashioned technique works on mirrors, too.

Make a 1:4 solution of white vinegar and water in a bucket. Squeeze a sponge out in it, then drag the sponge over the window from the top down. Rinse and repeat.

Working quickly to avoid streaking, polish the window with a dry microfiber cloth. Work as before, starting at the top and moving down.

15 MIN Kitchen speed-clean

Cleaning your kitchen from top to bottom is a task that could take you all day. But follow this speedy routine and you'll get all the important jobs done in just a matter of minutes—especially if you stay focused on the task at hand.

1 DEAL WITH DIRTY DISHES
Scrape unwanted food into the compost container or garbage can, then wash the dishes or load the dishwasher. If you're washing dishes by hand, leave the dishes to dry while you tackle the other jobs.

✓

2 TACKLE DIRTY PANS
Put away any clean saucepans and frying pans. Fill heavily soiled pans with hot water (use cold for remains of proteins, such as egg) and a squirt of dishwashing liquid, and leave to soak.

✓

3 WIPE THE STOVE
Wipe with a damp sponge and use a squirt of all-purpose cleaning spray to remove any stubborn stains.

✓

4 DON'T GET DISTRACTED
Try not to get distracted by reorganizing cupboards and drawers; instead, simply focus on putting things back where they belong.

✓

5 STORE FOOD AWAY
Store leftover food in suitable containers in the refrigerator. When you put food packages away in cupboards, check that they're securely closed.

✓

6 GATHER UP STRAY ITEMS
Using a basket, collect items that belong in other parts of the house and recruit a helper to put them back.

✓

7 WIPE COUNTERS AND TABLES
There's no need to get involved in thorough cleaning. Just wipe surfaces with a damp cloth and all-purpose cleaner, to gather up crumbs and wipe away any marks.

✓

8 DISPOSE OF GARBAGE
To reduce unpleasant smells, get rid of the garbage and line the garbage can with a new trash bag. Put any wine bottles, newspapers, and other recyclable items in the recycling.

✓

9 SWEEP THE FLOOR
Whizz around the kitchen floor with a broom to gather up a pile of dirt, then collect it with the dustpan and brush and throw it away.

✓

10 VACUUM THE FLOOR
If you still have more time once you've gotten rid of most of the crumbs and dust by sweeping, quickly vacuum the floor using the hard-floor attachment.

✓

5 MIN Clean the kitchen counter

Bacteria gather on kitchen counters, so keep them clean to prevent picking up a bug. At least once a week, follow this cleaning drill. There's no need to use an antibacterial spray; hot water and detergent will do the job.

BARE ESSENTIALS

dishwashing liquid

sponge

garbage can

all-purpose cleaning spray

microfiber cloth

→1

Before you start, clear the counter so the whole area is ready for wiping. Then fill a sink with hot water and add a squirt of dishwashing liquid.

→2

Gather any crumbs from the countertop using a sponge squeezed out in the soapy water, shake the crumbs into the garbage can, then rinse the sponge in clean water.

WHAT TO DO WHEN

DAILY → Wipe up crumbs and spills as you go to prevent a build-up of mess.

WEEKLY → Follow the steps below. Also wash all your kitchen cloths and sponges in hot soapy water and scrub the drain rack.

MONTHLY → Unplug countertop appliances and wipe them clean with a damp cloth.

Extra tips

To clean dirt from grouting on a tiled countertop, use a 1:4 solution of bleach applied with an old toothbrush.

Despite their durable appearance, granite and slate surfaces can scratch, so don't use an abrasive pan scourer to clean them.

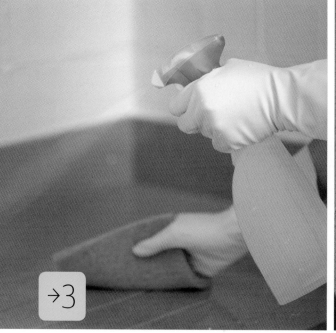

→3

Spray the counter with an all-purpose cleaning product, then wipe with the damp sponge, trying to remove as much cleaning-product residue as possible.

→4

Polish the counter using a clean, dry microfiber cloth. In addition to leaving the countertop shiny, this will remove any last traces of cleaning product.

Clean the kitchen floor

5 MIN

Kitchen floors get a lot of use and get dirty quickly, however, they usually only need to be thoroughly cleaned once a week. This fast mop-and-bucket technique will give you a spotless, germ-free floor in minutes.

BARE ESSENTIALS

vacuum cleaner
floorhead for hard floors
bucket with a mop-wringer
floor-cleaning solution
floor mop

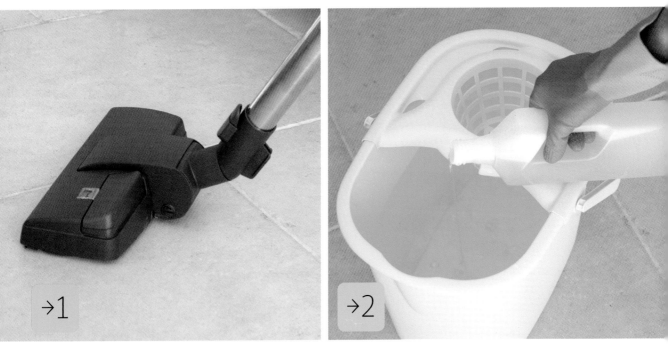

→1

Before you start to mop, get rid of surface dirt and crumbs by vacuuming the floor with the vacuum cleaner adjusted for hard floors, or by sweeping.

→2

Half-fill a bucket with warm water and add the recommended amount of floor-cleaning solution. Choose the correct type of solution for your floor.

ACTION PLAN

BEFORE YOU START → Clear any furniture out of the way to speed things up as you clean.

AS YOU WORK → Start at the far side of the kitchen and work toward the door. That way, you won't have to step on the wet floor.

AFTERWARD → Don't walk on the floor until it's completely dry, or you'll grind the dirt back in.

Extra tips

Use the technique shown here on laminate flooring, but be sure you wring the mop out thoroughly to prevent any damage to the finish. The mop should be almost dry.

If you have a stone floor, seal it regularly, following the supplier's instructions, or water will stain it.

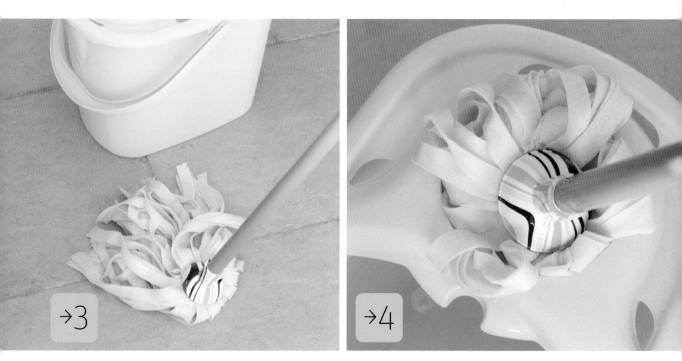

→3

Dip the mop in the bucket and wring it out thoroughly. Mop the floor using elongated oval strokes. Repeat until you have mopped the whole floor.

→4

If your floor-cleaning product should be rinsed off, refill the bucket with clean cold water. Use the technique in step 3 to remove all traces of soap. Let dry.

Oven kit

Whether you have a gas or electric oven, a fan or conventional one, the best way to keep it clean is to wipe it down with a damp cloth after every use. The same is true of microwave ovens. But there are always times when tougher measures are called for and that's when you need some supplies. Here is everything you need. If your oven is self-cleaning, your job is simpler—you only have to wipe away the ash residue.

PAPER TOWELS
Useful for applying baking-soda paste to a dirty oven.

SCOURER
Use to remove burned-on food from pan supports and from burners.

MIXING BOWL
Use when you are making your baking-soda paste.

BAKING SODA
Mildly alkaline, this cuts through greasy residues without the need for harmful chemicals. Mix it into a paste by adding a little water. Don't use on self-cleaning panels.

CREAM CLEANER
Useful for cleaning the exterior of the oven as well as electric plates with greasy residues.

OVEN CLEANER
A branded oven cleaner is useful for blitzing dirt from a neglected oven.

ALUMINUM FOIL
Use to line the bottom of your oven to save on cleaning time.

LAUNDRY DETERGENT
Good for soaking oven racks before you clean them.

DOUBLE-SIDED SPONGES
Wipe away crumbs with the sponge side; scrub burned areas with the abrasive side.

RUBBER GLOVES
Remember to wear these when using any oven-cleaning product.

10 TIPS Oven cleaning

If you've neglected your oven for ages and don't have the self-cleaning kind, you may need a chemical cleaning product to remove the grime. Follow the manufacturer's instructions carefully. These products can be hazardous.

1 READ THE INSTRUCTIONS
Many chemical cleaning products contain caustic soda, which can burn the skin, irritate the eyes, and harm the lungs. Keep the windows open and be sure to follow the directions on the product. ✓

2 WEAR RUBBER GLOVES
Wear rubber gloves for all stages, from applying the chemical cleaner to wiping it off. When you've finished, rinse the outside of the gloves with hot water. ✓

3 TAKE CHILDREN OUT
Consider going out when you leave the oven cleaner to do its work. This is especially important if you have young children, since it lessens the chance that they'll come into contact with the product. ✓

4 PROTECT THE FLOOR
Before applying the oven cleaner, spread newspaper on the floor under the oven to collect drips: the cleaning product may damage the floor. ✓

5 KEEP THE ROOM VENTILATED

Make sure you ventilate the kitchen well while you're cleaning the oven. Open windows—and doors, if possible, too.

6 PROTECT YOUR SKIN

Wear long-sleeved clothing and be careful not to splash the product on your skin. If you do, wash it immediately with soap and plenty of water.

7 PROTECT YOUR EYES

Chemical cleaners can irritate the eyes, so some manufacturers advise that you wear eye protection. If you get any in your eyes, rinse with plenty of water and see a doctor if they're still irritated.

8 CLEAN OVEN RACKS

Most products can be applied to oven racks as well as oven surfaces. If racks are particularly blackened, you may have to scrub them with a scourer before you wipe away the cleaning product.

9 USE DISPOSABLE CLOTHS

Wipe off the cleaning product with paper towels or with cloths that you can dispose of afterward.

10 REMOVE PRODUCT COMPLETELY

After you've removed most of the cleaning product, swap to a cloth rinsed in warm water. Use this to wipe the oven repeatedly until you're satisfied the product's all gone.

15 MIN Clean the oven

To clean a filthy oven, you have little choice but to turn to a branded oven-cleaning product. If the oven isn't too dirty, try this nontoxic alternative. Use it regularly, then you won't have to turn to chemicals.

BARE ESSENTIALS

nonscratch sponge

small mixing bowl

baking soda

paper towels

bucket

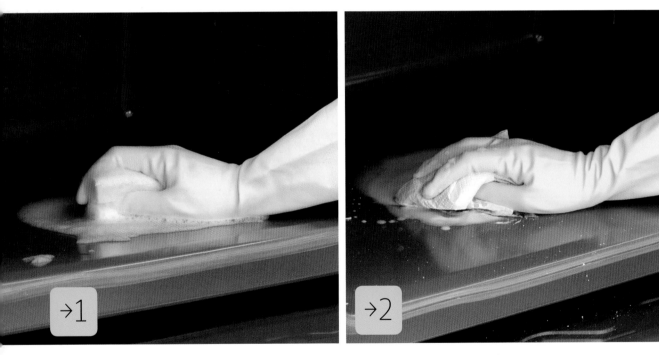

Using the soft side of a nonscratch sponge squeezed in soapy water, gather up any crumbs from the interior of the oven. Rinse the sponge and wipe again.

Make a paste by adding a little water to some baking soda in a bowl. Using some paper towels, coat the interior with the paste, then let stand, ideally overnight.

BEFORE YOU BEGIN

UNPLUG AN ELECTRIC OVEN AT THE OUTLET→ Water and electricity don't mix!

MAKE SURE THE OVEN IS COOL → If the oven's hot, wait until you can safely put your bare hands inside.

REMOVE THE RACKS → This gives you more room to maneuver. For how to clean the racks, see pp.50–51.

Using a chemical cleaner

When all else fails, use a branded oven-cleaning product (see pp.46–7). These are highly toxic, so read the instructions carefully. Be sure to protect your skin from splashes, open the window, and lay newspaper on the floor to catch any drips. Leave the product on for the recommended time, then rinse thoroughly.

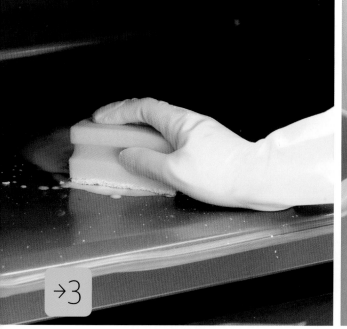

→3

Squeeze the nonscratch sponge out in clean warm water and use the abrasive side on the oven interior to scrub off any stubborn burned-on patches of food.

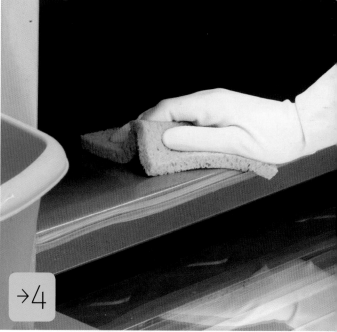

→4

Wring out a clean sponge in a bowl filled with warm water, then use to rinse away the scum and dirt. Rinse and wipe repeatedly until the oven is clean.

5 MIN Clean an oven rack

To clean off food that's stuck to an oven rack, the principle's the same as when cleaning a burned pan (see pp.112–13). Deal with the rack as quickly as possible and start by soaking it in laundry detergent.

BARE ESSENTIALS

laundry detergent

metal scourer

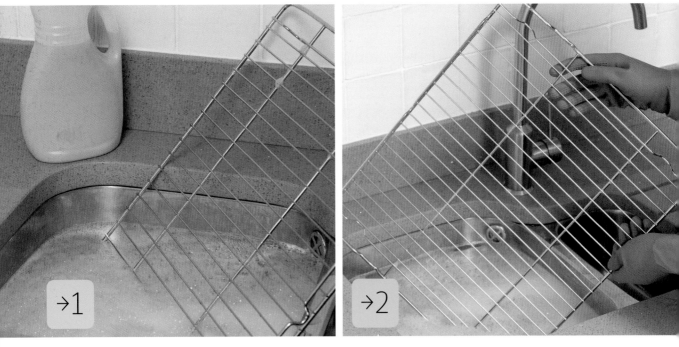

→1 **Fill the sink with hot water.** Add a capful of laundry detergent and submerge one rack at a time. You will probably have to lay it diagonally.

→2 **If you can only fit** half the rack in the sink, after 15 minutes, turn it around to submerge the other half. Leave for another 15 minutes.

WHAT TO DO WHEN

DAILY → When the oven is cool, remove what burned food you can from the racks with your fingers.

WEEKLY → When the oven is warm, quickly wipe the racks with a damp cloth to remove the worst of the grease and debris.

MONTHLY → Remove racks from the oven and clean them following steps 1–4 below.

Extra tip

If your oven racks are suffering from neglect, take them outside, spray with an oven-cleaning product, then put them inside a garbage bag. Leave for a couple of hours then rinse, preferably at an outdoor faucet. Finish by washing in warm soapy water in the sink.

→3

Use a metal scourer to scrub burned-on food from the bars of the half of the rack that was soaked first. Turn the rack around and repeat on the other half.

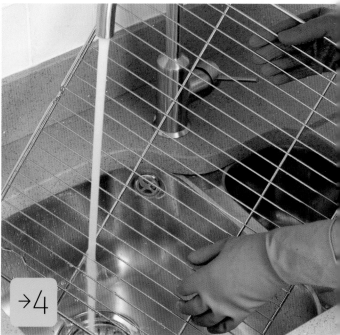

→4

Empty the sink and wash away the blackened debris from both sides of the rack under running water. Leave the rack to dry before replacing in the oven.

15 MIN Clean a refrigerator

To help keep your refrigerator clean and smells at bay, wipe up any food spills as soon as they occur. Then you'll only need to clean the interior thoroughly every couple of months. Wipe the exterior weekly.

BARE ESSENTIALS

dishwashing liquid, sponges

measuring cup

baking soda

spray bottle

wash tub

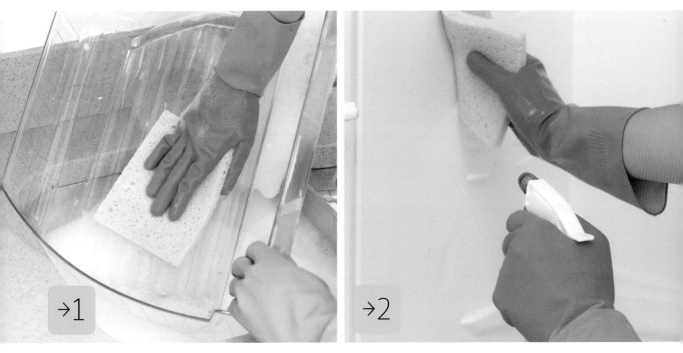

→1

Remove the shelves and drawers from the refrigerator and place them in a sink filled with warm water and a squirt of dishwashing liquid. Wipe them clean with a soapy sponge.

→2

Make a solution of 2 tsp baking soda and 1 quart (1 liter) warm water in a spray bottle. Use with a sponge to remove stains from the interior of the refrigerator.

BEFORE YOU BEGIN

TURN OFF AT THE POWER → Water and electricity are a dangerous combination.

EMPTY THE FOOD FROM THE REFRIGERATOR → Keep in a cool place or a cooler while you work.

VACUUM BEHIND → Pull the fridge out and vacuum the coils and fan with a dusting brush. Clean around the filter, if there is an ice-maker.

Extra tips

To keep the refrigerator fresh when you've cleaned it, sprinkle a teaspoon of baking soda onto half a lemon and place it inside the refrigerator. Replace every couple of weeks.

Don't use a scourer to clean the outside of the refrigerator. Stick to a soft sponge and an all-purpose cleaning spray.

→3

Fill a wash tub with warm water mixed with a squirt of dishwashing liquid. Apply the soapy water on a sponge to wipe clean the interior of the refrigerator.

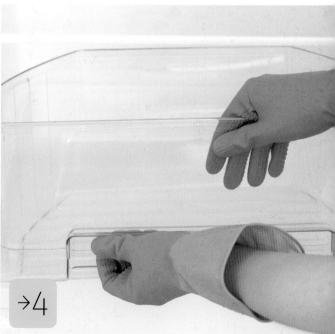

→4

Dry the shelves and drawers then replace them in the refrigerator. Finish by moving the refrigerator back into position, plugging it in, and replacing the food.

5 MIN Descale and clean a kettle

If your kettle's coated with limescale it won't boil efficiently. It can also affect the taste of hot drinks. This environmentally friendly descaling method works fast, whether for a stovetop or an electric kettle.

BARE ESSENTIALS

measuring cup

white vinegar

lemon

microfiber cloth

dishwashing liquid

→1

Make up a solution of equal parts white vinegar and water in a measuring cup. Fill the kettle with this solution, ensuring it's not so full that it bubbles over when it boils.

→2

Bring the kettle to a boil and leave to soak overnight or for a minimum of two hours. After soaking, pour the vinegar solution away.

WHAT TO DO WHEN

DAILY → Empty the kettle each evening so you always start with fresh water the next day.

WEEKLY → Wipe the outside of the kettle to remove streaks and stains every time you clean the kitchen counter.

MONTHLY → Follow the steps below to keep your kettle limescale-free.

Quick clean with descaler

Branded descalers are less "green" and can irritate skin and eyes, so use with care. Half-fill the kettle with water, bring to a boil, unplug (if electric), and stand in the sink. Gradually add the descaler. Leave for at least 30 minutes, then empty, rinse well with cold water, refill, boil, and empty again.

→3

Rinse the kettle thoroughly, refill with fresh water and boil again. Pour this water away. If there's a vinegary smell, fill it with fresh water again, boil, and pour away.

→4

Rub any marks on the outside with the flesh of a lemon, then wipe with a microfiber cloth squeezed out in warm soapy water. Rinse, then dry with a dry cloth.

3 MIN | Clean a stained mug

Coffee is a natural dye and tea contains tannins that stain, so it's not surprising to find unsightly marks on mugs and cups. Luckily, there's a speedy, environmentally friendly solution to stains.

BARE ESSENTIALS

baking soda

old toothbrush

nonscratch sponge

dishwashing liquid

→1

Sprinkle a little baking soda in the mug, then add enough boiling water to cover the stains. Leave to stand for at least 30 minutes.

→2

Pour the baking soda and water solution down the sink, then scrub the stains with an old toothbrush. Make sure you reach all the way down to the bottom.

WHAT TO DO WHEN

DAILY → Don't leave coffee or tea dregs in mugs. Wash as soon as possible after use with hot soapy water.

WEEKLY → Use a dishwashing brush to scrub any mugs that are starting to get stained.

MONTHLY → Identify any stained mugs and clean them following steps 1–4 below.

Extra tips

Fill the mug with a solution of equal parts boiling water and white vinegar. Leave overnight, then scrub with a nonstick sponge, wash, and rinse.

For the toughest stains, pour a teaspoon of bleach into each mug, then fill with boiling water. Let the mugs soak for 5 minutes, then rinse well.

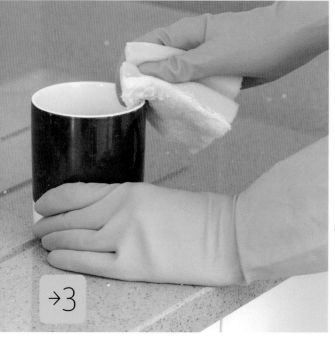

→3

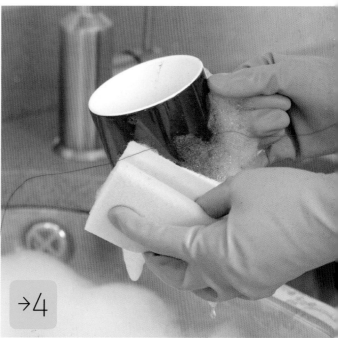

→4

If there are still any stains remaining that the toothbrush hasn't removed, rub them gently using the abrasive side of a nonscratch sponge.

Once you're sure all the stains are gone, finish by washing the mug with your usual dishwashing liquid and warm water. Rinse, dry, and put away ready for use.

Recycling kit

Much of the garbage you create in the kitchen can be recycled or composted. This will keep your garbage can from filling up too fast. If you compost, it will also help keep the garbage can clean, since you won't be putting food waste in it. Store your recycling containers in an easy-to-reach place so recycling doesn't feel like extra work. If you don't have space in the kitchen for the bulkier items, keep them in a utility area.

GLASS AND BOTTLE CONTAINER
Make sure it's sturdy and leak-proof and rinse items before putting them in.

PLASTIC-BAG HOLDER
To save space, look for one that's designed to be hung on the back of a cupboard door.

COMPOST CADDY
Collect food waste here and clean once a week to prevent flies and odors.

CONTAINER FOR CANS
Rinse cans before storing them. To save space, crush them with a can crusher.

CONTAINER FOR PAPER
Use exclusively for dry items, such as paper and cardboard, to keep them from becoming soggy. Flatten boxes before putting them in.

15 MIN Living room speed-clean

Although the living room can easily get cluttered, fortunately, the mess is usually superficial. It's nothing that 15 minutes with a damp cloth and a vacuum can't fix. Make sure you vacuum last to collect dust dislodged during cleaning.

1 LET IN THE FRESH AIR
Open the window to let in some fresh air. You could also light a fragranced candle or use a naturally fragranced air-freshener spray.

2 GET RID OF CRUMBS
You may not have time to vacuum sofas and chairs, but at least remove any crumbs by scooping them up in a barely damp microfiber cloth.

3 PICK UP AUDIOVISUAL EQUIPMENT
Put audiovisual equipment in its proper place. Don't leave CDs, DVDs, or games out of their boxes to gather dust.

4 WIPE THE TELEVISION
Use a barely damp microfiber cloth to remove any sticky fingerprints from the television screen.

5 PUT TOYS AWAY

Pile children's toys into a trunk or other large storage box and stow it in a corner. Wipe any grubby items with a damp microfiber cloth.

6 CLEAN THE MIRRORS

Use a barely damp microfiber cloth to clean any smears from the mirrors. Add a tiny drop of dishwashing liquid for stubborn marks.

7 CLEAR OFF SURFACES

Take glasses and mugs back to the kitchen, put books back on book shelves, and put magazines in the magazine rack.

8 STRAIGHTEN THE FURNITURE

Straighten sofas, chairs, and rugs. If you have throws, fold them and arrange them neatly on the backs of chairs and sofas or on armrests.

9 DUST QUICKLY

Use a damp microfiber cloth to tackle dust hotspots quickly, such as book shelves, picture frames, and lampshades.

10 FINISH BY VACUUMING

Vacuum the floor and rugs, focusing particularly on heavy-traffic areas like the doorway and in front of the sofa. If you have time, pull out the sofa and vacuum behind.

10 MIN Clean a washable wall

Clean your walls regularly and you'll never have to deal with a hard-to-remove build-up of dirt. Use this speedy method just once a year. Start by vacuuming to remove surface dirt, then the job's less messy.

BARE ESSENTIALS

vacuum cleaner

dusting-brush attachment

bucket

dishwashing liquid

large sponge, towel

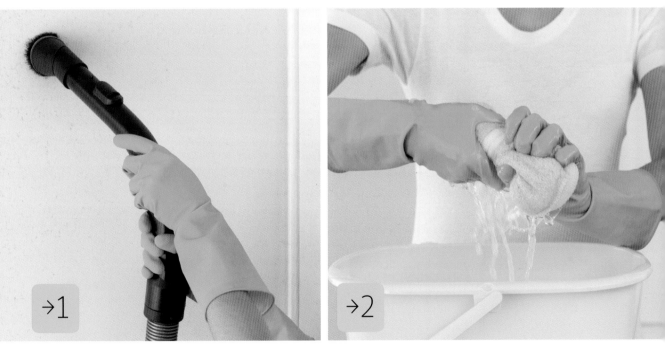

→1

→2

Before you start to wash, remove dust from the wall by vacuuming it with the dusting-brush attachment. Start at the top and work your way down.

Fill a bucket with warm water and add a squirt of dishwashing liquid. Wet the sponge in the water, then wring it out thoroughly so dirty drips don't streak the wall.

Extra tips

To clean a wallpapered wall, vacuum with the dusting-brush attachment (see step 1), then check if the paper is washable. To do this, carefully wet an inconspicuous area. If the color bleeds or fades, then you'll have to stop and accept that you can only vacuum the paper. If it proves washable, proceed, following steps 2–4 below.

To remove heavy grease from a washable wall, for example, from the area around the stove, make a solution of warm water and a handful of soda crystals. Wet a sponge in the solution, wring it out thoroughly, then use to wipe the wall. Rinse the sponge in clean water and wipe again to rinse off the solution. Repeat, if necessary.

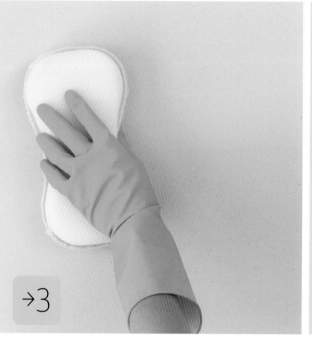

→3

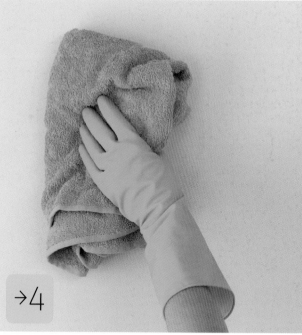

→4

Sponge the wall, starting at the top and working your way down. When one area is clean, rinse out your sponge and wipe the surface again to remove any dishwashing liquid.

Working as quickly as possible to prevent streaking, pat the wall dry using a towel. A very dirty wall might need to be cleaned twice once it has dried. If so, repeat steps 1–4.

5 MIN Clean a television

Like all electronic equipment, televisions generate static, which attracts dust—and dust can damage the components inside. It only takes a few minutes to dust and then clean the television, too.

BARE ESSENTIALS

vacuum cleaner with brush attachment

microfiber cloths

dishwashing liquid

→1

Unplug the television, then use the brush attachment on your vacuum cleaner and vacuum the back, paying special attention to the ventilation grilles.

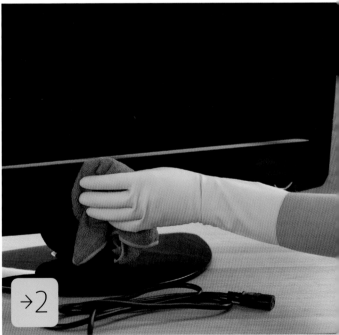

→2

Using a wet microfiber cloth that has been squeezed out thoroughly, wipe away any dirt and dust on the television casing, the wires, and the plug.

WHAT TO DO WHEN

DAILY → Quickly wipe the screen with a barely damp cloth to remove dust.

WEEKLY → Vacuum behind the television with the brush attachment.

MONTHLY → Wipe electronic equipment with a barely damp cloth. Include remote controls (see box, right), DVD players, and games' consoles.

Clean the remote control

Wipe with a damp cloth to remove dust. Make sure the cloth is well wrung out, since you must not get water inside.

Use a cotton swab squeezed out in warm water and a little dishwashing liquid, to remove any dirt from between the buttons.

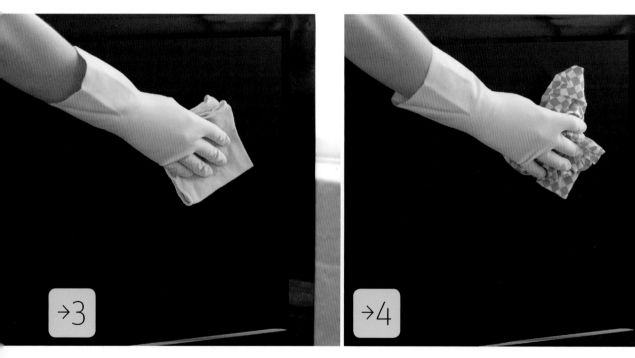

→3

Using another well-squeezed-out microfiber cloth with a dab of dishwashing liquid, gently remove any dirty marks from the television screen.

→4

Using a dry microfiber cloth with firm downward movements, gently buff the screen dry. Work quickly to avoid leaving streak marks on the screen.

10 MIN Polish wooden furniture

If you've got an old or special piece of solid-wood furniture, treat it carefully. This speedy wax will restore the shine and feed the wood. And the great thing is, you only need to do it once or twice a year.

BARE ESSENTIALS

small, soft, decorator's paintbrush

microfiber cloths

beeswax furniture polish

dust cloth

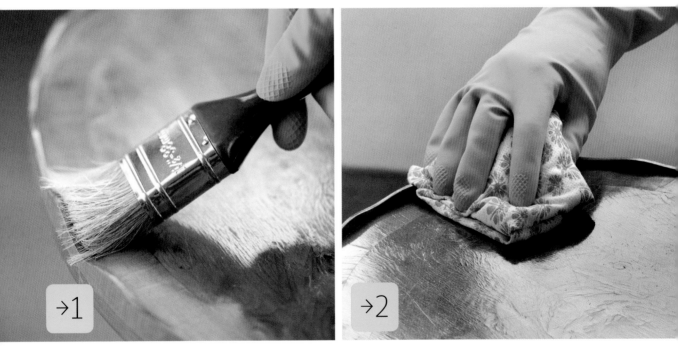

→1

→2

First, dislodge surface dust from any crevices or moldings on the furniture. The best tool for doing this is a small, soft, decorator's paintbrush.

Use a microfiber cloth to remove the rest of the dust. Make sure you have removed it all before applying polish or the dust will be ground into the wood with the polish.

WHAT TO DO WHEN

WEEKLY → Dry-dust (see pp.18–19) regularly to remove surface dust.

EVERY FEW MONTHS → If the surface is losing its gleam, buff it up gently using a clean dust cloth, as in step 4.

EVERY SIX MONTHS → Clean and polish once or twice a year by following steps 1–4 below.

Extra tips

To remove grease marks from wooden furniture, sprinkle the marks with talcum powder then cover with paper towels. Press down firmly and the paper will absorb the grease.

If damaged furniture is antique, don't repair it yourself; take it to a specialized restorer. This will prevent devaluation.

→3

Apply a small amount of beeswax furniture polish to a clean microfiber cloth, then apply to the furniture, wiping in the direction of the grain. Repeat as necessary.

→4

When you have applied a thin layer of wax to the whole surface, use a clean dust cloth to buff it gently. The surface should have a soft gleam when you have finished.

Remove scratches from a solid-wood floor

10 MIN

Polishing a solid-wood floor is a major job that you should do once a year with a rented polishing machine. In between polishes, keep your floor scratch-free with this simple, speedy technique.

→1

As soon as possible after you have spotted the scratches, remove any furniture that is in the way, and vacuum the area thoroughly using the head for hard floors.

→2

Gently rub the scratches with fine steel wool (grade 000) until you can no longer see them. Sweep away the dust left behind with a dustpan and brush.

Extra tips

To remove chewing gum, candle wax, or wax crayon from a wooden floor, cover the area with an ice-filled plastic bag, leave until the gum or wax has hardened, then carefully remove, using a blunt knife or the edge of a plastic card like a credit card.

You can't sand scratches on a wood-laminate floor as you can on a solid-wood floor because the surface of wood laminate often consists of nothing more than a photographic appliqué on top of a core of melamine and fiberboard. To remove scratches, use a special laminate repair kit.

To prevent scratches on wooden floors, always use cap castors on chair and table legs.

→3

Using a small spatula, carefully apply a little floor wax to the scratched area. Work the wax into the scratches by pressing on the spatula, Leave for 15 minutes.

→4

Using a clean dust cloth, thoroughly buff the area. Turn the dust cloth from time to time so you always use a clean part. Continue until you have a smooth, polished surface.

5 MIN Vacuum a sofa

Sofas are expensive and crumbs and dirt will damage their covers. Keep them in tip-top condition by vacuuming them every week. If you notice any stains, follow the stain-removal tips in Chapter 4.

BARE ESSENTIALS

vacuum cleaner

crevice nozzle

dusting-brush attachment

→1

Remove all pillows and seat cushions, and lay them on the floor. If your sofa stands next to the wall, pull it out so you can vacuum behind it.

→2

Check between the back and seat and down the sides for any items that may have fallen there, then vacuum in all the nooks and crannies using the crevice nozzle.

Cleaning upholstered furniture

Clean upholstered furniture about once a year, depending on how much use it gets. Don't wait until it looks dirty: by then the dirt will have started to damage the fabric.

If your furniture has fitted covers, call in a professional. The job will be done more quickly and the results will be better thanks to the professional equipment.

If you have loose covers, follow the manufacturer's instructions. You can usually wash them on a cool wash. Leave them to dry naturally to prevent shrinkage and put them back on the sofa while they're still damp—that way it's easier to get them back on.

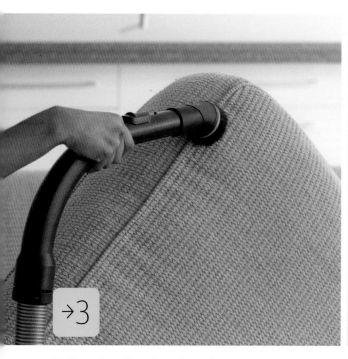

→3

→4

Using the dusting-brush attachment and gentle suction, vacuum the entire sofa, including the back and cushions. Focus especially on areas where dust gathers.

When you have finished, replace the seat cushions, plump the loose pillows, and put them back on the sofa. Move the sofa back into position.

20 MIN Polish a leather sofa

Although you should wipe up spills immediately and vacuum crumbs weekly, a leather sofa only needs to be well cleaned and polished once a year. Use soft saddle soap to do both jobs at the same time.

BARE ESSENTIALS

vacuum with brush attachment

microfiber cloths

soft saddle soap

dry sponge

dust cloth

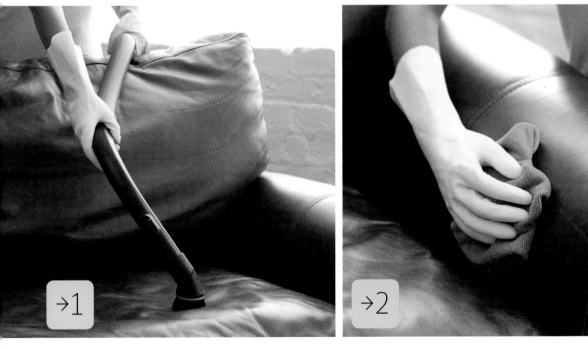

→1

Check down the sides of the sofa for any items that have fallen there, then vacuum the whole surface using the soft brush attachment.

→2

Wet a microfiber cloth in warm water and squeeze it out thoroughly so it is barely damp. Use this to wipe away any remaining surface dirt.

Extra tips

You can polish the leather with a leather-conditioner spray, but note that these only polish. They don't clean.

To remove water-based stains, dab them immediately with a soft white cloth or paper towels. Leave to dry thoroughly and if the mark's still visible, buff the area with a clean dry cloth.

To remove greasy stains, treat with a solution of soap flakes or use soft saddle soap, then rinse with clear water. Always make sure you don't overwet the leather.

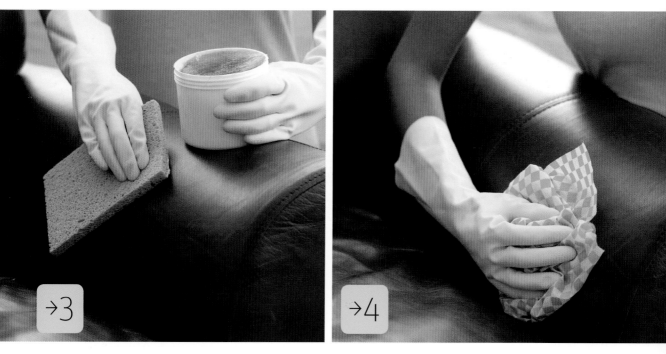

→3

→4

To remove ingrained dirt and nourish the leather at the same time, apply soft saddle soap on a dry sponge, working on a small area at a time. Rub in the saddle soap well.

Finish by rubbing the entire surface of the sofa with a clean, dry microfiber cloth. Use a firm repetitive motion to bring a glow to the leather.

Polishing kit

The polishing kit you need depends on the items you have to polish. Traditional beeswax polish is best for wooden furniture and floors. Silicone polishes don't fill small scratches as beeswax does, and it can make surfaces slippery. Brass, copper, and silver ornaments need to be polished from time to time to keep tarnish at bay.

MICROFIBER MITT
Use a mitt rather than a cloth for quickly dusting large surfaces like tables and cupboard fronts. Microfiber can be machine-washed but it's better not to use fabric softener.

METAL POLISH
Some products suit several different metals, but check before use.

MICROFIBER CLOTHS
Use to remove dust quickly and efficiently before you start to polish. Microfiber is electrostatic so attracts dust like a magnet.

DUST CLOTH
The traditional soft cloth used for dusting. Now that there are microfiber cloths, you may prefer to save it just for buffing up surfaces after polishing.

DECORATOR'S BRUSH
A handy tool for getting rid of surface dust from moldings on furniture.

TOOTHBRUSH
Use an old one to ease dust out of moldings and intricate details on ornaments.

OLD TOWEL
Use when polishing small items to protect the surface you're working on from the polish, which may damage it.

BEESWAX POLISH
This is the gentlest wax for feeding and shining solid wood. You only need to apply it once or twice a year.

RUBBER GLOVES
Always wear gloves when polishing furniture and metals to protect your hands from the polish.

15 MIN Bedroom speed-clean

Keep your bedroom and dresser fresh and neat. Run through this speed-clean checklist at least once a week, and you'll cover every aspect of the room, from the bed to the waste-paper basket and from the mirrors to the floor.

1 LET IN THE FRESH AIR
Even in winter, let some air into the bedroom by opening a window. This will help to keep it smelling fresh, and will reduce humidity and keep it cool, both of which deter dust mites. ✓

2 AIR THE BED
Try to air the bed first thing every morning. When you get up, turn the comforter or top sheet and blankets back over the foot of the bed. ✓

3 DAMP-DUST
Wipe washable surfaces with a damp cloth, particularly bedside tables, where dust may have gathered around lamps, books, and other items. ✓

4 MAKE THE BED
When the bed has aired for at least 30 minutes, make the bed and plump the pillows. If you have a bedspread, throw it over for that hotel-bedroom look. ✓

5 CLEAN THE MIRRORS

If mirrors are smeared, wipe them clean with a barely damp microfiber cloth. If stubborn marks remain, repeat, adding a tiny drop of dishwashing liquid to the cloth.

6 RETURN ITEMS TO THE CORRECT ROOM

Remove mugs or other kitchen items that have found their way into the bedroom, along with anything else that doesn't belong there.

7 EMPTY THE WASTE-PAPER BASKET

Empty the waste-paper basket, separating any items that can be recycled and putting the rest with the household garbage. Line with a clean trash bag.

8 PUT CLOTHES AWAY

Sort out clothes that are lying around, putting like with like, then shake them out and hang them up in the closet, or fold and place in the drawer.

9 STOW COSMETICS AND OTHER PERSONAL ITEMS

Store items away neatly in covered baskets or bowls to minimize dusting. Remember that anything left on show will only gather dust.

10 FINISH BY VACUUMING

Focus on areas where there is heavy traffic, like the doorway and alongside the bed. Use the crevice nozzle in the corners. If there's time, pull out the bed and vacuum behind.

4 MIN Change the sheets

Change your bed linen once a week—and more frequently in hot weather. There's no need to struggle to put on comforter covers and pillowcases if you follow these simple steps.

BARE ESSENTIALS

comforter and comforter cover

fitted bottom sheet

pillows and pillowcases

→1

Remove the dirty bedding and pile the comforter and pillows nearby. Pull on a clean fitted bottom sheet, pull it tight over the corners, and smooth out any wrinkles.

→2

Turn a pillowcase inside out, reach into the corners, grab the corners of a pillow, then roll the pillowcase down over the pillow. Arrange the pillows on the bed.

Extra tips

Comforters are easier to look after than blankets and you can make the bed in moments. The main choice is between down, feather and down, and synthetic fillings. Goose down is the best insulator, but is more expensive. Down is sometimes combined with duck feathers to reduce the cost. Synthetic fillings—usually polyester hollow fiber—are best for allergy sufferers.

Most comforters with natural fillings must be professionally laundered, but you can launder comforters with a synthetic filling yourself (see pp.148–9).

Pillows come with the same fillings as comforters. In addition, you can buy latex-filled pillows, which keep their shape well, and are good for people with allergies.

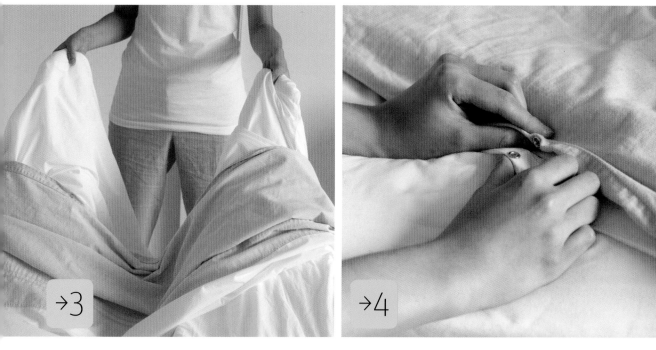

Lay the comforter cover on the bed. Push a corner of the comforter into a top corner of the cover; do the same with the other corner. Now pull the cover down.

When the comforter is fully inside the cover, hold the cover and the comforter together, and shake the comforter flat. Fasten the bottom opening of the cover.

2 MIN Make the bed

Get into the habit of making your bed every morning as soon as you get up. It only takes a minute or two—excluding airing time—and will freshen up the bed, helping to get rid of dust mites and flakes of dead skin that you have shed during the night.

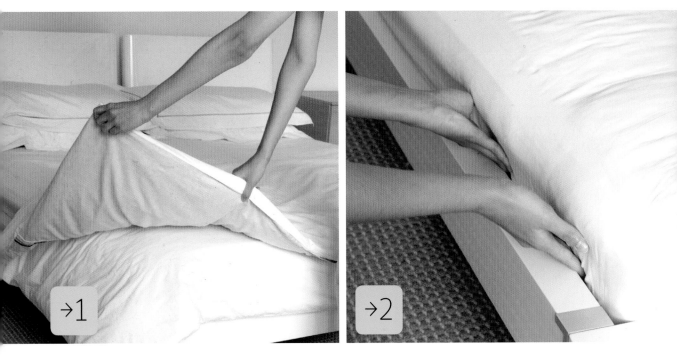

→1

→2

As soon as you get up, fold the comforter back on itself and lay it at the foot of the bed. Leave it so that it airs while you get dressed and ready for the day.

At least 30 minutes later, dust the bottom sheet with your hand and smooth it down. Fit it back tightly over the corners of the mattress, then tuck it in well at the sides.

Extra tips

If you have blankets and a flat bottom sheet, start by following step 1 below, and air the bed by folding back the blankets and the top sheet instead of the comforter. Now smooth the bottom sheet. Next, unfold the blankets and the top sheet, keeping them together, then fold back the top edge of the sheet. Move to the bottom of the bed. Tuck the sheets and blankets in firmly along the bottom, then lift the sides (again keeping sheets and blankets together) and fold them back on top of the bed. You'll now see a corner hanging down. Tuck this in, then drop the sides back down and tuck those in. You should now have a neat miter—a hospital corner.

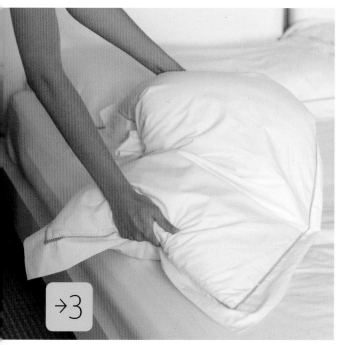

→3

Plump up the pillows, since these will have been flattened in the night. Lay them neatly at the head of the bed, turning them around so that last night's top edge is at the bottom.

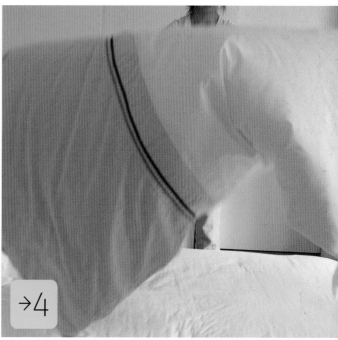

→4

Finally, use a brisk upward motion to shake the comforter and let it fall back onto the bed. Now straighten the comforter out, making sure it covers the bed evenly.

10 MIN Maintain your mattress

Vacuum your mattress every six months, sponge off stains and, if it's a spring mattress, turn it over. These simple steps will extend the life of the mattress by years and will keep dust mites at bay.

BARE ESSENTIALS

vacuum cleaner

dusting-brush attachment

handwash laundry detergent

sponge

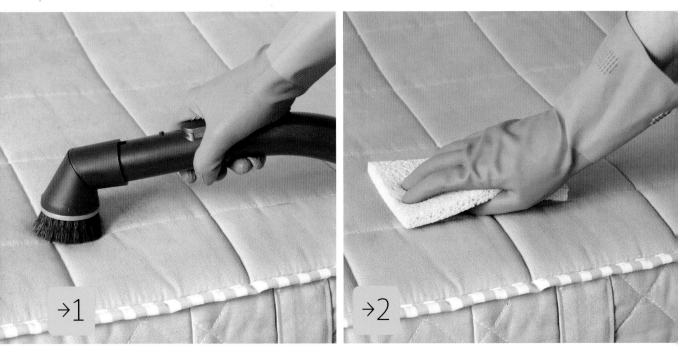

→1

→2

Remove the mattress protector then vacuum the mattress using the dusting-brush attachment. Work the brush well into the stitching to help remove dust mites.

Squeeze out a sponge in a solution of warm water and handwash laundry detergent and use to scrub away stains. Sponge with clean water to remove the detergent.

Extra tips

Always use a mattress protector on top of your mattress, since it's more hygienic. Launder it—together with pillow protectors (another essential)—monthly.

In addition to turning a spring mattress over, you should also turn it from end to end. Turn it over every 6 months and from end to end after another 6 months.

You don't have to turn latex and memory-foam mattresses over, but you should still rotate them from end to end to maximize their lifespan. Do this once a month.

To combat the smell from any urine stains, dab the stains with a 1:4 solution of white vinegar to water. Finish by dabbing with a clean, dry cloth.

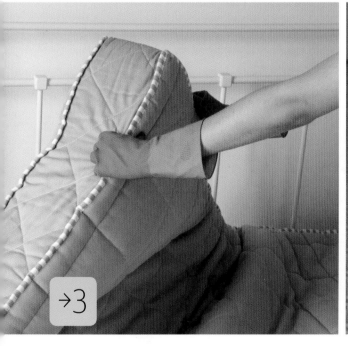

→3

Leave the mattress to dry, then turn it over. If you want to speed up the drying process, use a warm hairdryer. Vacuum the other side and sponge off stains there, too.

→4

When the second side has dried, replace the mattress protector with a clean one. You are now ready to make up the rest of the bed, following steps 1–4 on pp.78–9.

Bathroom kit

Keeping the bathroom clean is important for hygiene reasons. Clean messes up quickly each time you leave the bathroom and you'll only have to spend a few minutes each week cleaning the floor and changing the towels. You don't need an extensive cleaning kit, but do keep it separate from the cleaning materials you use in the rest of the house.

TOILET BOWL CLEANER
The angled neck on the bottle makes it quicker and easier to squirt the cleaner inside the toilet, particularly under the rim of the bowl.

PAPER TOWELS
Useful for wiping the exterior of the toilet; it's hygienic, since you can throw the paper away afterward.

SPRAY CLEANER
The spray speeds up the job of disinfecting the exterior of the toilet bowl.

CREAM CLEANER
Use to remove most marks from the bathtub and sink quickly.

BATHROOM SPONGE
The abrasive side deals speedily with stubborn marks on the sink, bathtub, and shower.

VINEGAR SOLUTION
Spray in the sink, bathtub, and around the shower to prevent limescale.

RUBBER GLOVES
Reserve a special pair for cleaning the toilet.

Bathroom speed-clean

5 MIN

You can achieve this bathroom speed-clean in just 5 minutes if you gather the appropriate cleaning materials in a bucket before you start work. Keep this toolkit ready in a bathroom cupboard for future use.

1 VENTILATE THE ROOM
Either open a window or turn the extractor fan on while you follow the rest of the steps. Good ventilation prevents damp and mildew.

2 WIPE THE SINK
Using a barely damp cloth, wipe behind the faucets and around the sink to remove any soap scum. Empty and wipe the soap dish if it's full of soapy water.

3 WIPE THE BATHTUB
Using a barely damp cloth, wipe the bathtub to remove soap scum, hair, and other dirt. Wipe up water from behind the faucets and remove hair from the drain.

4 DRY THE SHOWER CURTAIN OR SCREEN
If the shower curtain's wet, open it fully, shake it out, wipe it dry, and leave it open. If you have a shower screen, wipe it dry.

5 CLEAN THE TOILET

Wipe the seat with a piece of paper towel, then spray or squirt disinfectant toilet-bowl cleaner into the bowl, especially around the rim. Once a week, clean the outside of the bowl and the handle.

6 CLEAN THE MIRRORS

Clean any smears from the mirrors using a barely damp microfiber cloth. If there are stubborn marks, remove them with a tiny drop of dishwashing liquid.

7 STRAIGHTEN UP THE TOILETRIES

Store like with like, putting as many items as possible away in the bathroom cabinet or in drawers. If you leave them out on display, they'll gather dust.

8 CHANGE TOWELS AND WASH CLOTHS

Once a week, replace dirty towels and wash cloths with clean ones. If you have a full machine load, wash them right away, but if not and they're not dry, leave to dry before putting in the laundry hamper.

9 CLEAN THE FLOOR

Sweep the floor to remove dust and fluff. At least once a week, mop with a floor-cleaning product, focusing on the area around the toilet.

10 EMPTY THE GARBAGE CAN

Empty the garbage can, separating any items that can be recycled and putting the rest with the household garbage. Line with a clean trash bag.

3 MIN Clean the bathroom sink

Bathroom sinks get a lot of use and can harbor germs. This swift cleaning takes just minutes. Get into the habit of doing it after every use, and you won't need to spend any time cleaning the sink more thoroughly.

BARE ESSENTIALS

double-sided bathroom sponge

cream cleaner

spray bottle

white vinegar

microfiber cloth

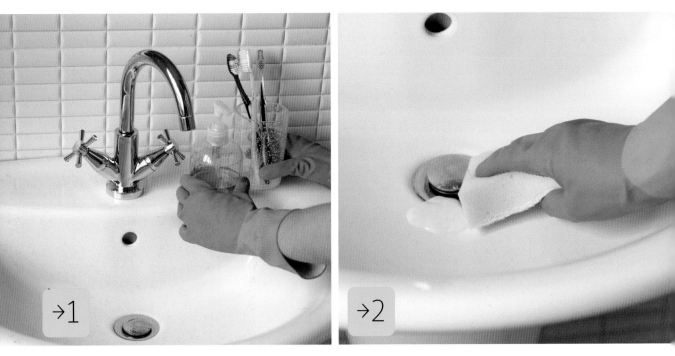

→1 **Clear clutter from around** the sink, then fill with hot water and leave for a minute to loosen any soap scum. Wipe the sink with the sponge, then let the water drain away.

→2 **Use the abrasive side** of the sponge and some cream cleaner to remove any marks, especially from the drain, the overflow, and around the base of the faucets. Rinse well.

WHAT TO DO WHEN

DAILY → Wipe the sink down after every use to keep it free of soap scum.

WEEKLY → Clean the sink and faucets thoroughly following steps 1–4.

MONTHLY → If there's a limescale build-up, soak paper towels in white vinegar, lay it on the limescale, and leave until the limescale is soft and you can wipe it away.

Extra tips

Clean a stone sink with a soft cloth and a neutral or alkaline cleaning product. Use a specialized stone-cleaning product for persistent stains, and to prevent stains, use a stone-sealant once a year.

Use an old toothbrush to clean hard-to-reach areas such as behind the faucets.

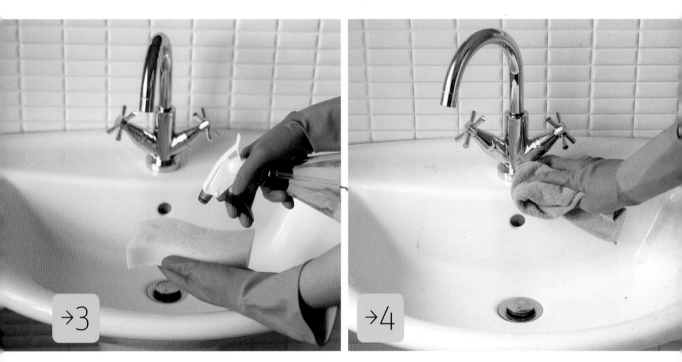

→3 **To minimize any build-up** of limescale, mix equal parts of white vinegar and water. Spray the solution onto the sponge, wipe around the sink and faucets, then rinse.

→4 **For a sparkling finish,** dry the sink with a clean, dry microfiber cloth. Use this to polish the faucets and drain, too. Drying helps to prevent limescale deposits.

5 MIN Clean the bathtub

Take a few moments to wipe out the bathtub after every use, and it will only take minutes a week to clean it thoroughly. If you wait until there's an old, dried-on ring, it will take a lot longer to restore the bathtub's sparkle.

BARE ESSENTIALS

double-sided bathroom sponge

cream cleaner

spray bottle

white vinegar

microfiber cloth

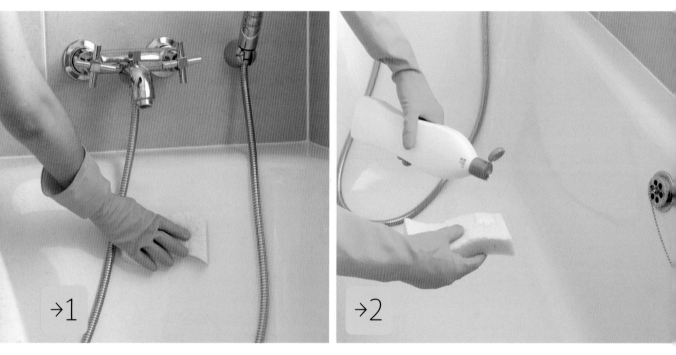

→1

→2

Using a damp sponge, wipe around the bathtub to pick up soap, hair, and other dirt. Wipe away water on the edge of the bathtub or behind the faucets. Rinse well.

Apply cream cleaner to any stains or marks, using the abrasive side of the sponge. Leave the cleaner to work for 10 minutes, then rinse well.

Extra tips

If your bathtub's been neglected and is badly stained, fill it with hot water, add a scoop of laundry detergent, and leave it overnight. The next day, let the water out, then wipe around with a sponge. The stains and soap scum should disappear.

To clean mold from the sealant around the bathtub, use a fungicidal spray. Once the sealant's clean, reapply it regularly to prevent the mold from reappearing.

To remove scratches from an acrylic bathtub, rub gently with metal polish then clean the tub thoroughly. Never use an abrasive cleaner or an abrasive sponge, since these will scratch the surface.

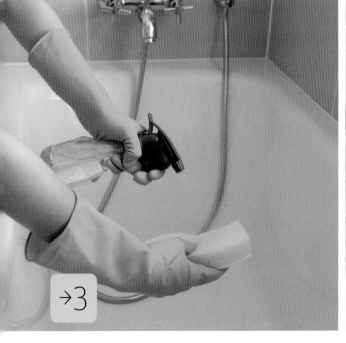

→3

To prevent a build-up of limescale, mix equal parts of white vinegar and water. Spray the solution onto the sponge and wipe the bathtub, including the faucets.

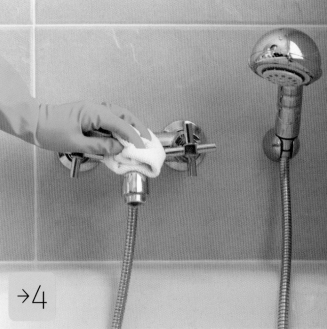

→4

Rinse the bathtub thoroughly, then finish by wiping the faucets and any other chrome parts. First, use the soft side of the sponge, then polish with a dry microfiber cloth.

5 MIN Clean the shower

The main enemy of showers is limescale, but you don't have to use a branded product to wage war. Keep it under control in just a few minutes a week with this simple, environmentally friendly routine.

BARE ESSENTIALS

double-sided bathroom sponge

spray bottle

white vinegar

microfiber cloth

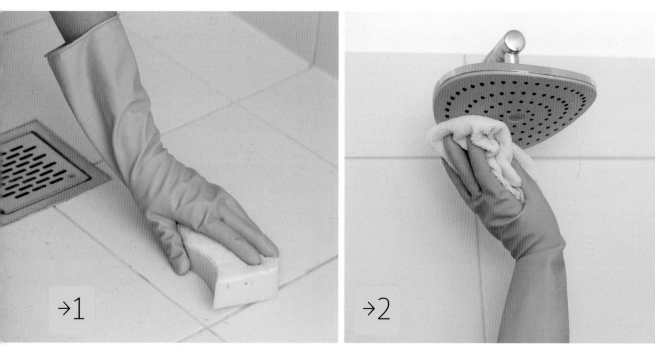

→1

→2

Start by wiping down the walls and floor of the shower stall using the soft side of a damp bathroom sponge. Be sure to wipe away any pools of water.

Mix equal parts of white vinegar and water in a spray bottle and use to spray the shower head and any other metal parts. Rinse, then polish with a dry microfiber cloth.

Extra tips

To keep a shower curtain clean, wash it regularly on a hot wash using biological detergent. If it's badly mildewed, soak it for 10 minutes in a solution of 1 part household bleach to 4 parts water before you machine-wash. Alternatively, scrub the mildew with a paste made from baking soda and water, then rinse in plenty of clean water. A final solution if the curtain is heavily mildewed is to spray it with a branded mildew remover, following the manufacturer's instructions.

To clean mold and mildew from grouting, scrub with a solution of 1 part bleach to 3 parts water or with a paste made from baking soda with a couple of drops of white vinegar or bleach.

→3

Next, tackle the door to remove smears and any build-up of limescale. Do this by spraying with the vinegar-and-water spray, then rinse with a damp sponge.

→4

Finish by drying the door using a clean, dry microfiber cloth. Work quickly to avoid streaking. If the door has any metal trim or a metal handle, dry those, too.

3 MIN Clean the toilet

Toilets are breeding grounds for bacteria. Destroy them with a speedy, weekly cleaning. If several people use the toilet, also clean it daily with a squirt of branded toilet cleaner from an angle-necked bottle.

BARE ESSENTIALS

disinfectant toilet cleaner

paper towels

toilet brush

spray bottle

white vinegar

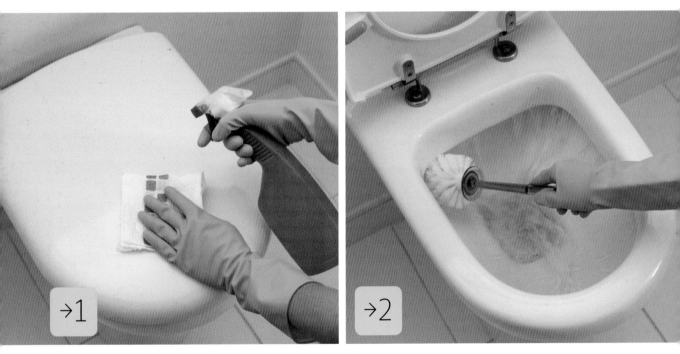

Spray a disinfectant toilet cleaner around the inside and outside of the toilet bowl. Leave the inside to soak for a few minutes while you wipe outside with paper towels.

Clean the bowl with the toilet brush, especially under the rim. Flush the toilet and while it is flushing, use the brush to rinse away any remaining disinfectant.

Extra tips

To remove a heavy build-up of limescale in the toilet, remove most of the water from the bowl using a plastic cup (see step 2, p.96), then pour in white vinegar to cover the stains. Leave until the stain has gone, then flush to wash the vinegar away. Alternatively, use a branded limescale-removing product, following the manufacturer's instructions.

You can use household bleach inside the toilet bowl as an alternative disinfectant, but don't leave it to soak for more than 30 minutes or you risk damaging the porcelain.

Never mix different toilet-cleaning products. They contain chemicals that may react together to produce toxic gases.

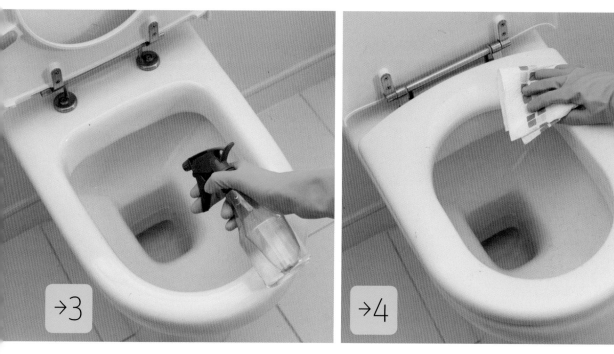

To prevent limescale or treat a mild build-up, mix equal parts of white vinegar and water in a spray. Spray generously in the toilet bowl and leave to soak for 10 minutes.

Flush the toilet one more time to wash away the vinegar. Finish by wiping the seat well with paper towels to soak up any splashes.

10
MIN

Unblock a toilet

When your toilet gets blocked, try to stay calm and see if the blockage clears itself. If it doesn't, put on your rubber gloves, gather your tools together (see box, right), and try this speedy remedy.

BARE ESSENTIALS

newspaper

plastic cup

bucket

plunger

bleach

→1

Lay newspaper down around the toilet bowl to protect the floor from any splashes. Start by trying to pull out any visible obstruction with your hands.

→2

If that doesn't unblock the toilet, you'll have to use a plunger. Begin by emptying most of the water from the toilet bowl using a plastic cup. Pour the water into a bucket.

Extra tips

When you're faced with a blocked toilet, you often have the urge to keep on flushing the toilet in the hope that this will clear the blockage. It won't. You'll simply end up with a flooded floor.

Prevent a blocked toilet in the first place by only throwing toilet paper in the bowl.

Never try and flush disposable diapers, tissues, sanitary napkins, or tampons. Also, train everyone in the household to use only small quantities of toilet paper with each flush. Even an excess of toilet paper can cause a blockage.

If all else fails, call a plumber.

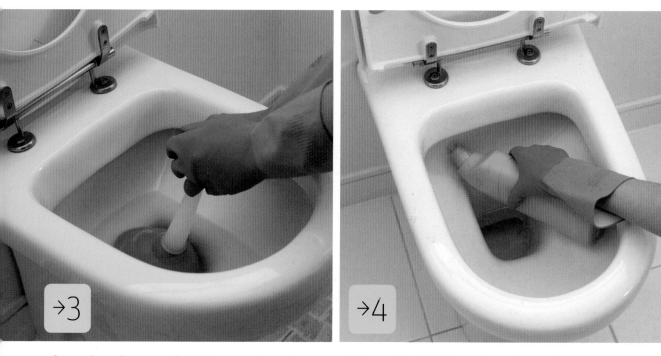

→3 **Place the plunger tightly** over the toilet outlet. Press it down firmly, then quickly lift it up and press it down. You may need to pump up and down like this up to 10 times.

→4 **When the blockage** has cleared and the water level has fallen, flush the toilet, then squirt a small amount of bleach around the rim to disinfect the bowl.

5 MIN Home office speed-clean

Whether your home office is a desk in your bedroom or an entire room, it will need regular attention to keep the area uncluttered and dust-free. Follow these steps once a week and you'll feel much more on top of your work space.

1 BRING IN THE FRESH AIR
Open windows to bring in some fresh air or, if that's not possible, light a fragranced candle or use a naturally fragranced air-freshener spray.

2 RETURN ITEMS TO THE CORRECT ROOM
If there are empty coffee cups or plates around your desk, take them to the kitchen. Return stray items from other rooms to their rightful places.

3 STRAIGHTEN UP THE DESK AREA
Before you can dust and clean your desk, you need to organize it. Put paperwork in a pile ready to file, put books and magazines on shelves, and put away pens, pencils, notebooks, and other odds and ends.

4 CLEAN THE DESK
Using a damp cloth and a squirt of all-purpose cleaner, wipe around the desk to remove any sticky marks or stains.

5 SPEED-CLEAN THE KEYBOARD

Turn the keyboard upside down and shake out the dust and crumbs, then wipe with a barely damp microfiber cloth to remove dirt and grubby fingerprint marks.

6 CLEAN THE COMPUTER SCREEN

Using a dry microfiber cloth, quickly buff the screen and remove any dust that has collected on or around it.

7 WIPE THE PHONE

Wipe the phone with a barely damp microfiber cloth and at least once a month, dampen a cloth with disinfectant spray and wipe the handset.

8 ARRANGE CORDS AND CABLES

Check that cords and cables are tucked away along the baseboard or behind your desk, and that they're not cluttering up the desk area.

9 CLEAN THE CHAIR

Wipe your office chair with a damp cloth to pick up any hair and surface dirt. If there are stains, spend a moment tackling them with an upholstery-cleaning product.

10 FINISH BY VACUUMING

Vacuum the floor, focusing on heavy-traffic areas such as the doorway and the area under your desk.

10 MIN Clean a laptop

A laptop quickly gathers crumbs, hair, dust, and dirt. These harbor bacteria and could affect the laptop's performance. This cleaning only takes minutes and will keep your laptop in good working order.

BARE ESSENTIALS

microfiber cloths

spray can of compressed air

cotton swabs

→1

Unplug the laptop before you begin and remove any peripherals. Close the lid, then wipe the outer casing with a barely damp microfiber cloth.

→2

Open the laptop then, from about 6in (15cm) away, carefully spray compressed air around the keyboard, air vents, ports, and CD/DVD slot.

BEFORE YOU BEGIN

TURN OFF THE LAPTOP AND UNPLUG IT
→ Water and electricity don't mix!

DON'T RUSH → Hurry at your peril. You risk
causing damage.

REMOVE ALL PERIPHERALS → These include
the mouse, printer cable, keyboard cable,
and anything plugged into a port or slot.

Extra tips

If you don't have a can of compressed
air, use a hair dryer on its coolest
setting to blow dust away from air
vents and from the keyboard.

You could also use a soft paintbrush
for dislodging dust, and antistatic
wipes for cleaning the screen.

→3

→4

Dampen a cotton swab in warm water,
squeeze it well, and use between the keys
to remove marks and dirt. Finish by wiping
with a barely damp microfiber cloth.

Using a dry microfiber cloth, wipe
surface dust off the screen, then dampen
the cloth very slightly and wipe again.
Finish by buffing with a clean, dry cloth.

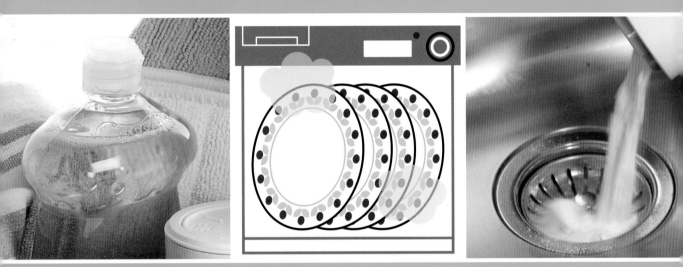

Doing dishes

Dishwashing kit

If you don't have a dishwasher or are trying to cut down on using yours, then you'll have to do dishes by hand. But you don't want to spend ages at it. The speedy way to get a stack of clean dishes is to use the right supplies, and here is what you need. Keep it all on hand near the sink, and you'll have clean dishes in a jiffy.

DOUBLE-SIDED SPONGES
Be sure to use a nonscratch sponge on nonstick pans.

SOAP-DISPENSING SCOURER
Fill the handle with dishwashing liquid and you have a quick and easy way of doing dishes when you only have one or two dirty items.

CUTLERY DRAINER
Stand one on your drain board to hold cutlery after it has been washed. For safety, put knives blade-end down, but forks and spoons dry better handle-end down.

DISH TOWELS
Wash regularly in a hot wash cycle and use a clean one for every batch of dishes you do.

WASH TUB
Useful in preventing scratches in your sink and for doing glasses.

SCOURERS
These quickly remove most burned-on food. Choose a plastic scourer to clean a nonstick pan.

DISHWASHING LIQUID
Don't use too much: a squirt is all you need for a sinkful of water.

DISHWASHING BRUSH
Use to clean food from the tines of forks. Be sure to wash in hot water from time to time.

DRAIN RACK
Save drying time by air-drying your dishes on a rack standing on the drain board.

RUBBER GLOVES
Always wear these to stop your hands from drying out as you do dishes.

SPONGE
Use to clean glassware.

4 MIN Prepare to do dishes

Doing dishes doesn't have to be horribly time-consuming. For speed and efficiency, spend a minute or two setting things up first. And remember that you need clean tools for the job and plenty of hot water.

BARE ESSENTIALS

dishwashing liquid

sponge

dishwashing brush

pan scourer or nonscratch sponge

→1 **Fill food-encrusted pans** with enough hot water to cover the food. Add a squirt of dishwashing liquid and leave to soak while you continue with the rest of the preparation.

→2 **Clear the drain board** and sink of clutter by removing any dirty dishes that have been piled in the sink or any clean items left on the dish rack.

BEFORE YOU BEGIN

IF YOU CAN'T DO DISHES RIGHT AWAY →
Rinse items so the dirt doesn't harden.

DON'T POUR OILS AND FATS DOWN THE SINK → They'll block it. Instead, pour into an old jar, and when it's full, throw it away.

SOAK PROTEIN DEBRIS LIKE EGG, MILK, AND OATMEAL IN COLD WATER →These respond best when soaked in cold water.

Loading the dishwasher

Scrape off large food particles and unless dishes are only lightly soiled, rinse quickly before loading. They'll emerge cleaner and it helps avoid nasty smells while you wait for a full load.

Load matching items near each other. It makes for faster unloading and putting away.

Scrape food from the plates into the garbage and stack the dirty dishes on the counter by the sink, roughly in the order that they will be washed (see pp.108–9).

Fill one sink with hot water and add a squirt of dishwashing liquid. Fill a second sink or dishwashing bowl with hot water ready for rinsing the clean dishes.

10 MIN Do the dishes

The quickest way is to start with cleaner, delicate items and move onto heavier, dirtier ones. That way, the water stays cleaner for longer. As you work, check that every item is clean before you move on to the next.

BARE ESSENTIALS

dishwashing liquid

sponge

dish rack

dishwashing brush

pan scourer or nonscratch sponge

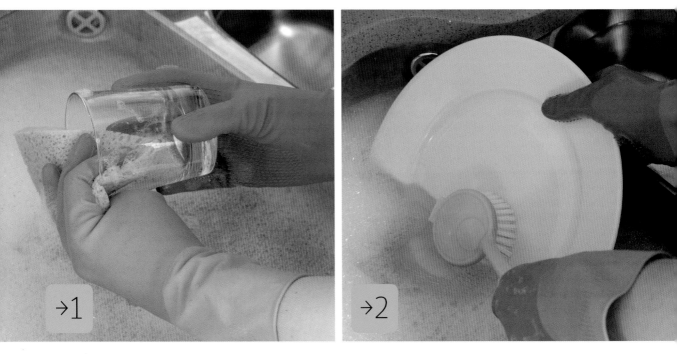

→1

Start by washing the glassware with a sponge. Be gentle to avoid breakages, then dip in the hot rinsing water and place, bottom up, on the dish rack.

→2

Next, wash the cleanest plates, followed by the dirtier ones. Change the water if it gets oily. Use a dishwashing brush, then rinse in the hot water before draining.

ACTION PLAN

BEFORE YOU START → Really hot water gives best results, so wearing gloves is a must.

AS YOU WORK → Change the water when it gets oily, especially when you're washing a big load.

AFTERWARD → Rinse the sink with hot water and a drop of dishwashing liquid.

Extra tips

Air dry The best method of drying the dishes is to leave items on a dish rack or on the drain board.

Towel dry If you prefer to use a dish towel, make sure it's clean so as not to spread bacteria onto your clean dishes and cutlery.

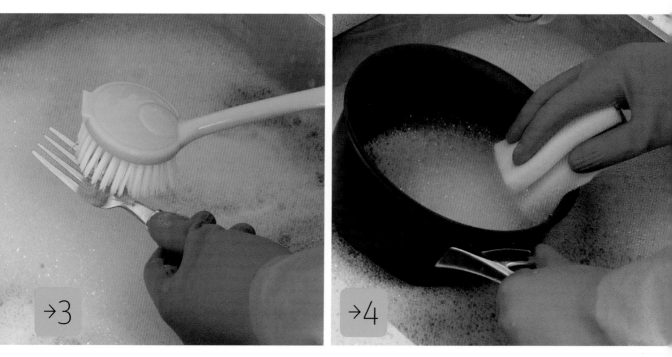

Now move on to the cutlery. Use the dishwashing brush to make sure you clean all the food off the tines of the forks. Dip in the hot rinsing water and let drain.

Scrub pots and pans with a pan scourer or a nonscratch sponge if you are cleaning a nonstick pan. Rinse each item in hot water before standing it on the rack to drain.

10 MIN Make glasses sparkle

Glasses often develop a white haze in the dishwasher. If the glass has been "etched"—slightly dissolved by alkaline detergent—it's irreversible. If it's just limescale deposit, the acid in vinegar will help remove it.

BARE ESSENTIALS

dishwashing liquid

rinsing bowl

white vinegar

sponge

dish rack

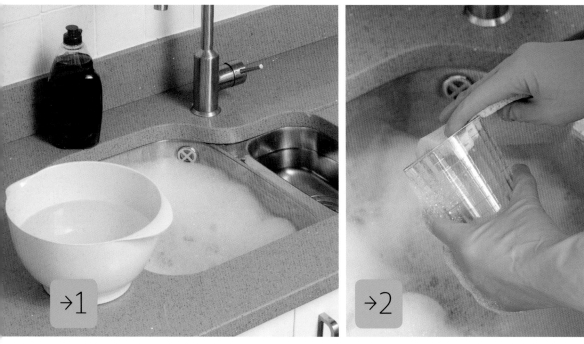

→1

→2

Fill a sink with hot water and a drop of dishwashing liquid, and a second sink or a dishwashing bowl with white vinegar and water (1:8). Fill a third bowl with hot water.

Wash one glass at a time in the soapy water, using a sponge. Pay special attention to the rim of the glass where smudges and marks build up.

BEFORE YOU BEGIN

PUT ON RUBBER GLOVES → That way you can use really hot water, which will get your glasses cleaner.

USE A PLASTIC BOWL → If glasses are precious or delicate, it prevents damage.

USE A LARGE BOWL FOR THE VINEGAR SOLUTION → You must be able to roll your largest glass in it.

Extra tip

Borax is another all-around cleaner that produces good results on glassware but without the vinegary smell. Make a solution of 1 teaspoon of borax to 1 quart (1 liter) of hot water, then follow the instructions below, using the borax solution in step 3. Be sure to rinse well, since borax shouldn't be ingested.

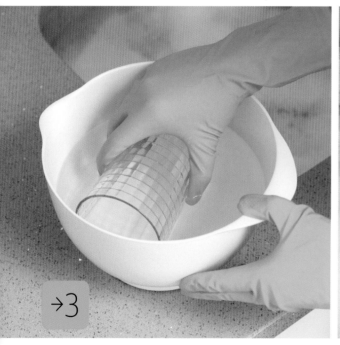

→3

Now roll each glass in the bowl containing the vinegar solution. Dip the top of the glass in first, then the bottom, or stem, if it's a wine glass.

→4

Finally, rinse the glass in the hot water to remove the vinegar. Stand it bottom up on a dish rack or on a clean dish towel on the drain board.

Pan-maintenance kit

Keep pans in tip-top condition by always cleaning them right after use. That way there won't be a build-up of dirt and grease that takes ages to get rid of. Most dirty pans can be cleaned in a minute or two if you have the right equipment. When you're faced with burned-on food, simply leave the pans to soak for a while.

DISHWASHING LIQUID
Your first defense against greasy pans. Today's products cut through grease fast.

THIN CLOTHS
Useful for placing between nonstick pans when they're stacked on top of each other in a cupboard.

SCOURER
Use to clean stainless-steel pans after you've soaked them in some soapy water.

BAKING SODA
A good, environmentally friendly alternative to using chemical cleaning products.

MICROFIBER CLOTHS
Use to remove greasy marks from the outside of stainless-steel pans.

PAPER TOWELS
A very quick (occasional) cheat for cleaning nonstick pans when they're only lightly soiled.

LEMON JUICE
Used with salt, it's a quick, environmentally friendly way to clean copper pans.

RUBBER GLOVES
Wear rubber gloves when cleaning pans to protect your hands.

SALT
Use with lemon juice for cleaning tarnish from copper pans.

5 MIN Clean a burned pan

When you have to deal with food that's stuck to the bottom of a saucepan, don't waste time trying to scrape it off. The job will only take minutes if you soak the pan as quickly as possible.

BARE ESSENTIALS

wooden spoon

baking soda

scourer

dishwashing liquid

dishwashing brush

→1

Scrape loose bits of food into the compost caddy or into an ordinary garbage can. Use a wooden spoon or spatula, or a plastic spatula if it's a nonstick pan.

→2

Sprinkle some baking soda onto the burned-on food, then add enough hot water to cover the dirty areas. Leave to soak for at least an hour.

BEFORE YOU BEGIN

PUT ON RUBBER GLOVES → These will protect your hands at every stage.

REMOVE ANY WOODEN UTENSILS → Don't leave the pan to soak with a wooden spoon in it, since the spoon might swell and crack.

CHECK YOUR MATERIALS → Avoid using metal scourers or harsh abrasive cleaning detergent on a nonstick pan.

Extra tip

After you have removed any loose bits of food (see step 1 opposite), pour a little laundry detergent in the pan. Half-fill with cold water, bring to a boil, and simmer for 15 minutes, or until the burned-on food loosens. Then remove it with a spoon or spatula, rinse, and dry.

→3

Using a metal scourer or a plastic one if it's a nonstick pan, work to dislodge the remaining burned-on food. You should find that all the debris comes away.

→4

Discard the debris, then wash the pan as normal, using hot water, a squirt of dishwashing liquid, and a dishwashing brush. Leave the pan to dry.

10 TIPS Using a dishwasher

There's nothing more frustrating than finding grubby items in the dishwasher after a wash cycle. A dishwasher works like a shower. Its fixed jets only spray the surfaces they can reach. That's why how you stack items affects how well they're washed.

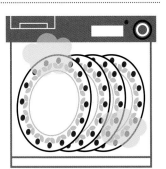

1 SKIP RINSING
There's no need to rinse items before loading unless food has dried on them. In this case, rinse to soften the food, then scrub it off. Otherwise, just scrape food off into the garbage.

✓

2 PUT THE RIGHT ITEM ON THE RIGHT RACK
Items on the lower rack get a hotter, more intense wash, so put heavily soiled things here, including pots and pans. Stack glassware, cups, and more delicate items on the top rack.

3 LOAD CUTLERY CORRECTLY
Load with some handles facing upward and some down. This stops cutlery from nestling together, which may mean it doesn't get so clean. Some dishwashers have cutlery shelves that prevent this from happening.

4 DO NOT LET ITEMS TOUCH
The idea is to load as much as you can without letting the items touch, or there's a risk they won't get clean. And always, check that the spray arm at the bottom is free to rotate.

5 CHECK ITEMS ARE DISHWASHER-PROOF

Don't put rubber utensils, many nonstick pans, anything with a printed or painted pattern, and wooden items such as spoons and cutting boards in the dishwasher. These should be hand-washed.

6 FILL UP THE RINSE AID

Keep the rinse-aid compartment full. A small amount of rinse aid is released during the final hot rinse to help reduce smears.

7 DO NOT WASH ON THE HOTTEST CYCLE

There's no need to choose the hottest cycle. It will cost you and the environment more and can damage glassware. For hygienic cleaning, all you need is a wash cycle that's at least 126°F (52°C).

8 RINSE THE FILTER

Most new dishwashers have self-cleaning filters but if you have an older model, you may need to remove and rinse the filter regularly to get rid of food debris. Check the manufacturer's instructions.

9 FILL UP THE SALT

Even if your dishwasher tablets contain salt, you still need to fill the reservoir with granular salt every month, especially if you live in a hard-water area. The salt activates the machine's water softener.

10 RUN A MAINTENANCE WASH CYCLE

Every couple of months, run a hot wash cycle with an empty machine and a dishwasher-cleaning product. This removes grease and limescale from all parts of the dishwasher, including those you can't see.

3 MIN Make a sink sparkle

The kitchen sink is a breeding ground for bacteria, so it should be thoroughly cleaned and disinfected at least once a week. Always wear rubber gloves for the job, so you don't splash bleach on your skin.

BARE ESSENTIALS

bleach

old toothbrush

nonscratch sponge

→1 **Make sure the sink area** is free of dishes, then fill the sink with hot water until it's almost overflowing. Add a capful of bleach and leave to soak for a few minutes.

→2 **The overflow is where dirt** often collects. Splash a little of the bleach solution down the overflow, then scrub it thoroughly using an old toothbrush.

WHAT TO DO WHEN

DAILY → Wipe the sink after every use, especially around the faucets and overflow.

WEEKLY → Follow steps 1–4 below to disinfect the sink thoroughly.

MONTHLY → Put your dishwashing brushes and scourers in the bleach solution to disinfect them, or throw them out and replace them.

Extra tips

For porcelain sinks, swap the bleach solution for warm soapy water to keep from dulling the surface, and rub any stains with baking soda.

If you use a wash tub, wipe it with a sponge soaked in the bleach solution every week, when you clean the sink thoroughly.

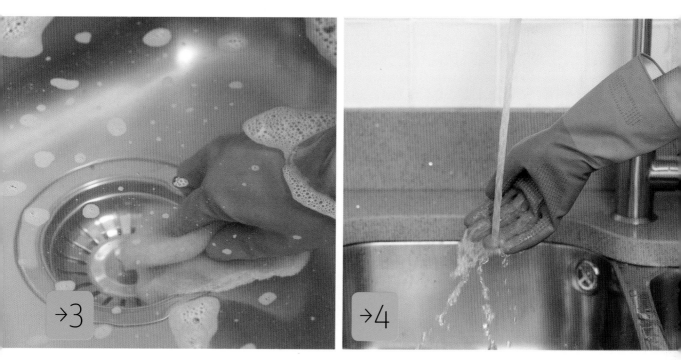

→3

With the bleach solution still in the sink, scrub away any stains on the sink using a nonscratch sponge. Stains most often form around the drain.

→4

Leave to soak for 1 hour or overnight, then let the water out of the sink. Rinse the sink thoroughly to be sure you remove all traces of bleach.

5 MIN Clear a slow-draining sink

A slow-draining kitchen sink is a sign of a blocked drain pipe. The most likely causes are grease, fat, and food debris. It usually only takes a few minutes to solve the problem and you shouldn't need chemicals.

BARE ESSENTIALS

baking soda

white vinegar

plunger

bleach

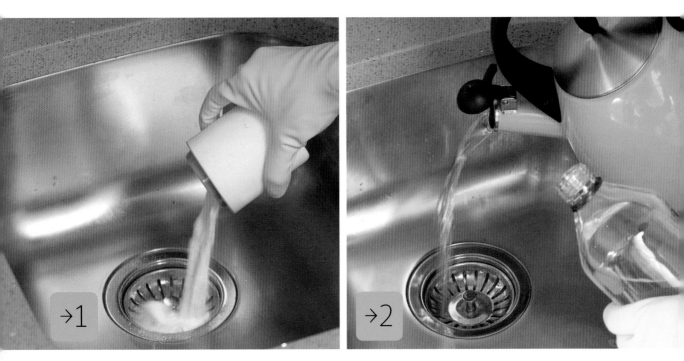

→1

Start by sprinkling 3–4oz (80–100g) baking soda down the drain, then wash it down with 1 cup (240ml) boiling water.

→2

If the blockage persists, pour ½ cup (80–100ml) white vinegar down the drain, then flush with a full kettle of boiling water.

WHAT TO DO WHEN

DAILY → Clean any food debris from the drain and rinse well.

WEEKLY → Pour a full kettle of boiling water down the drain to prevent a build-up of debris in the drain pipe.

MONTHLY → Pour a cupful of white vinegar down the drain to dissolve minor blockages.

Extra tips

Another way of dissolving grease is with soda crystals. Pour two cups of soda crystals over the drain then slowly pour in a kettle of boiling water.

If all these methods fail, try a chemical drain-unblocking product. Remember that these are caustic, so wear rubber gloves and rinse the sink well afterward.

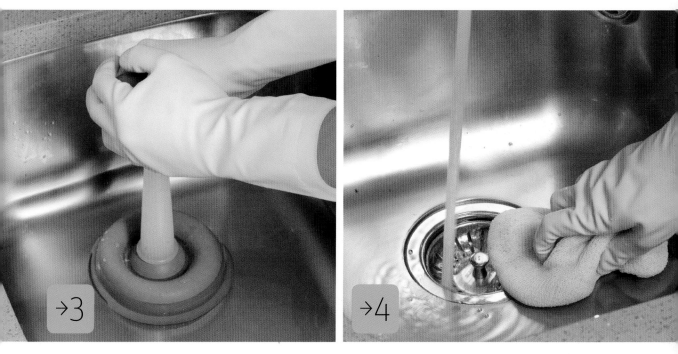

→3

Make sure there's 1–2in (2½–5cm) water in the sink, then cover the drain with a plunger. Pressing down firmly, pump up and down several times.

→4

When the blockage has cleared, rinse the sink and disinfect it with a little bleach. If the problem remains, try a drain-clearing chemical or call the plumber.

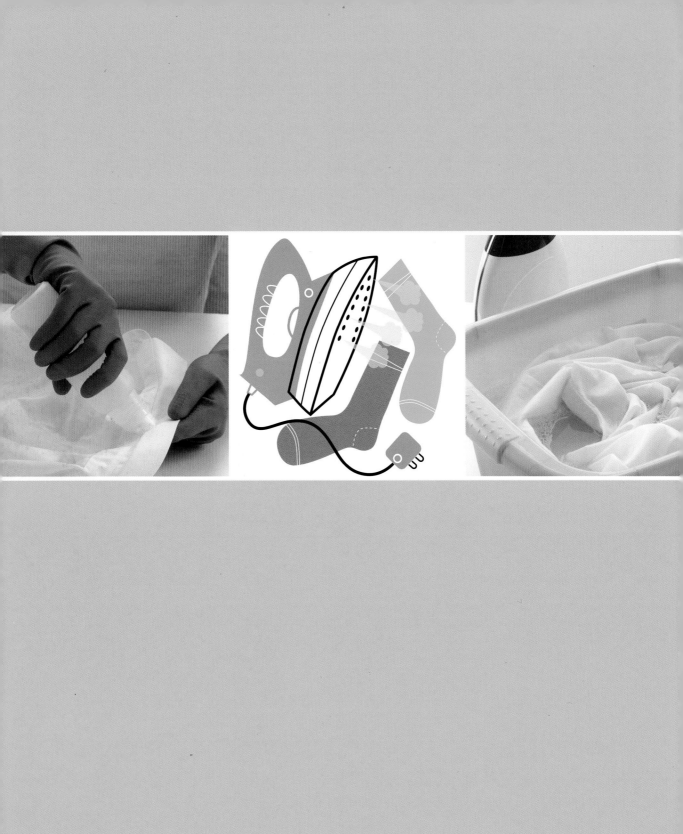

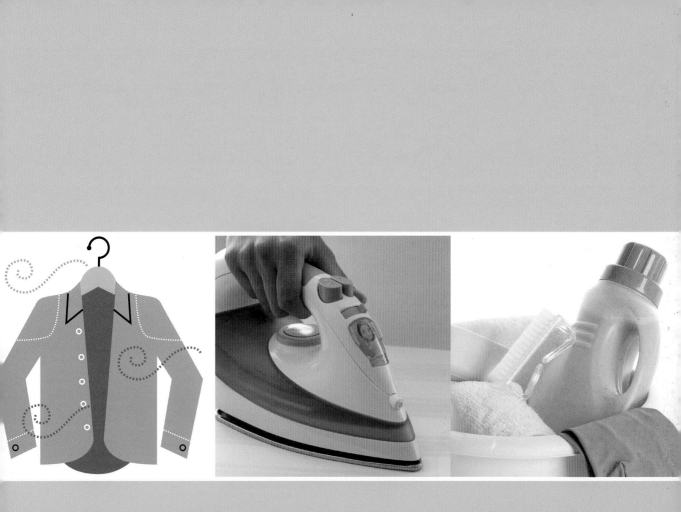

Clothes and laundry

5 MIN Sort the laundry

The key to preventing laundry disasters is to sort your laundry rigorously according to the manufacturer's care labels (see opposite). Some items are made of several fabrics and may include zippers or buttons. The recommendation on the care label takes this into account.

→1

Start by removing from the laundry basket any items labeled as hand-wash only. These will include silk, fine linen, some woolen items, and special lingerie.

→2

Divide the remaining laundry first according to the care label, then according to color. Make different piles for whites, dark colors, and bright colors.

LAUNDRY CARE LABELS

 WASH The numeral indicates the maximum temperature for washing.

 WASH A line underneath indicates the need for reduced agitation.

 HANDWASH If no temperature is specified, use the lowest or cold.

 DRY CLEAN Letters in the circle indicate the type of dry-cleaning agent.

 **DRY FLAT** Lay on a towel on a flat surface or on a mesh rack over the tub.

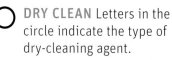 **DO NOT TUMBLE DRY** If there's no cross, you can safely tumble-dry.

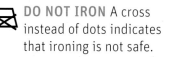 **DO NOT BLEACH** If there's no cross, you can use any type of bleach.

COOL IRON The number of dots indicates the ironing temperature.

DO NOT IRON A cross instead of dots indicates that ironing is not safe.

→3

Make sure that you empty pockets of tissues (these disintegrate and pieces will end up on the rest of the wash) and loose change, which may damage the machine.

→4

Turn dark items inside out to help preserve their color and do the same to T-shirts with applied designs. Also make sure you fasten zippers and buttons.

5 MIN Wash your whites

Don't be tempted simply to throw whites in the machine. A few minutes spent sorting them properly and dealing with stains means you won't have to soak them for hours to restore their good looks.

Start by sorting the true whites from the pastels. Be ruthless and don't include pale pastels or grays. You should put these in a separate wash for light colors.

Before you launder shirts and blouses, work a stain-removing product into the collar area. Collars often collect grime, especially along the fold.

MONTHLY SCHEDULE

DAILY → Check white items for stains and treat with a suitable stain-removing product as soon as possible.

WEEKLY → Sort through the laundry basket and remove the whites for washing. Then follow steps 1–4 below.

MONTHLY → Tackle graying items, following the tip in the box on the right.

Extra tips

Soak graying whites for 2 hours with the recommended amount of stain-removing detergent and 1½oz (40g) borax per quart (liter) hot water. Squeeze out, then wash as hot as possible.

Calcium deposits in the water can make your clothes turn gray, so add a capful of water softener to your wash.

→3

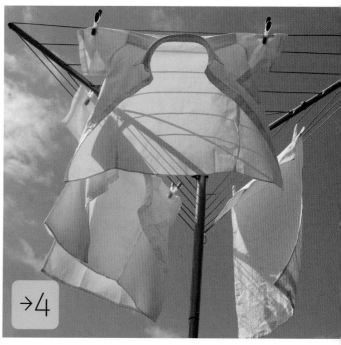

→4

Add a capful of laundry detergent to hot water in a wash tub and leave the items to soak for 1 hour. Then machine-wash at the hottest recommended temperature.

Dry your whites outside in the sun. Sunlight is a natural whitener so, unless you live in a heavily polluted area, drying your whites outdoors gives the best results.

Washing-machine maintenance

10 TIPS

Like other appliances, a washing machine will benefit hugely from a little TLC every few months, especially if you use it frequently. Following these tips doesn't take long and will save you time in the long run, since your machine will work efficiently.

1 DO NOT OVERFILL
Tempting as it is to pile as much as possible into the drum, you must leave room for the water and for the washing to move around. Always follow the manufacturer's recommendations on load sizes.

✔

2 AIR THE DRUM
Make sure you leave the door open after you've used the machine to let the drum air and dry properly. This will prevent mildew.

✔

3 CLEAN THE SEAL
Wipe the rubber door seal regularly with a clean damp cloth. This is where dirty scum builds up and causes an unpleasant smell, especially if you wash at low temperatures and use liquid detergents.

✔

4 CLEAN THE DETERGENT DISPENSER DRAWER
Remove the detergent drawer every few months and wash it in warm water. Don't forget to remove any build-up of soap beneath the drawer.

✔

5 WIPE THE EXTERIOR

Clean the casing regularly using a mild non-abrasive cleaner or gentle dishwashing liquid and water on a well wrung-out cloth. Wipe dry with a soft cloth.

6 CLEAN THE FILTER

Depending on the model of your machine and its age, you may need to clean debris regularly from the filter. Consult the manual to see if it's necessary and if it is, how to do it, and how often.

7 RUN A MAINTENANCE WASH

Regularly run an empty maintenance wash using the cottons program. This is especially important if you mostly wash at low temperatures, since it prevents the build-up of soap and limescale deposits in the machine.

8 ADD WASHING SODA OR VINEGAR

When you run a maintenance wash, put a cupful of washing soda or white vinegar in the detergent drawer to help clear any limescale.

9 REMOVE LIMESCALE FROM THE DRAWER

If there's limescale at the back of the detergent drawer, use an old toothbrush soaked in white vinegar to scrub it away. If the deposit is heavy, remove the drawer and soak it in a vinegar-and-water solution.

10 TURN OFF AT THE WATER VALVE

If you're going away on vacation or are leaving the machine unused for a period of time, turn it off at the water valve. This could prevent a leak in your absence.

Handwash kit

Sometimes handwashing is the only option. You may need something washed quickly, you may not want to put a delicate item in the machine, or hand-washing may be advised on the care label. Whatever the reason, always hand-wash in a dedicated plastic bowl or in the bathroom sink rather than in the kitchen. It's more hygienic that way.

STAIN-REMOVAL BAR
Use on damp fabric to remove stains from items before washing.

STAIN-REMOVAL LIQUID
Like the stain-removal bar (see above), you can use this on damp fabric to remove stains from items before washing. Some also incorporate a brush.

WASH TUB
Keep a bowl or tub specially for hand-washing. A tub used for dishes may be greasy from food deposits.

NAILBRUSH
Use with detergent to quickly shift grubbiness from shirt collars, cuffs, and underarm areas.

HANDWASHING DETERGENT
Specially formulated to be gentle.

TOWEL
Roll up woolens and other delicate items in a light-colored towel to remove excess moisture. It cuts down on drying time and protects the fabrics from damage caused by squeezing.

RUBBER GLOVES
Wear to protect your hands from the drying effects of detergents.

10 MIN Handwash clothing

Today's washing machines can cope with most fabrics, so if you check your clothing's care labels, you'll probably only need to handwash one or two special items (see opposite). The good news is that with delicate clothes, the less you do, the better the result. Just follow the speedy steps below.

Fill a tub with warm, not hot, water and add a capful of hand-wash detergent while the water is running. If color bleeds when you add the garment, wash it on its own.

Dab any stains with a suitable stain-removing product and gently rub fabric against fabric once or twice to loosen the stain. Rinse and repeat if the stain persists.

Extra tips

Silk garments must be washed by hand. Wash quickly in very cold water with a mild detergent and rinse in cold water, too. You can add a little hair conditioner to the final rinse to keep the silk soft and supple.

Wash cashmere quickly by hand in cool water with a very mild detergent. Don't squeeze or wring and rinse in cool water.

Dry flat once you have squeezed out excess water by rolling in a towel.

Handwash vintage clothing made from cotton, linen, and wool mixed with nylon or acrylics. Wash one item at a time in lukewarm water with a mild detergent. Don't wring or scrub, but pat between your palms, allowing the water to run through.

→3

→4

Wash the item by squeezing the soapy water through a couple of times. Never wring or stretch, especially woolens and items with beading, lace, or embroidery.

Rinse in clean water and repeat until the water is clear. Squeeze out gently in a towel to speed up the drying process, then dry, following the instructions on the care label.

10 TIPS Indoor drying

Drying laundry indoors is a must if you don't have an outdoor clothsline or a tumble dryer. You'll need to be inventive though to ensure that your home doesn't end up damp and/or draped with slow-drying clothes for days on end.

1 CHOOSE THE RIGHT DRYING RACK
Indoor drying racks can hang from the wall or ceiling, or they can be free-standing. Choose one that you can position in a warm but well-ventilated spot and move it into the sunlight if possible.

2 AVOID RADIATORS
Don't dry clothes on top of radiators. The clothes will get stiff and may shrink. It also causes condensation and reduces the warmth given out by the radiator.

3 OPEN THE WINDOW
Open a window while you're drying clothes indoors. This prevents condensation, which can lead to damp and mildew.

4 REMOVE EXCESS WATER
Before hanging your clothes to dry, make sure that you've removed all the water you can, otherwise they'll dry slowly and will start to smell damp (see tip 10).

5 SHAKE WELL
Before you hang clothes indoors to dry, give each item one short, sharp shake. This helps prevent wrinkles.

6 ORGANIZE THE DRYING RACK
When arranging clothes on a drying rack, put smaller items, such as underwear and socks, lower down on the rack and leave the upper tiers for larger and longer items like jeans and pants.

7 SPACE CLOTHES WELL
Space clothes out properly on the drying rack so air can circulate around them. This prevents them from drying slowly, which will make them smell damp even when they're dry.

8 USE HANGERS
Dresses, shirts, and jackets are best dried on hangers to preserve their shape and minimize wrinkles. Start by hanging them in the shower or over the bathtub while they're dripping, then move them to a drying rack.

9 DRY WOOL FLAT
Woolen items need to be dried flat or they'll lose their their shape. Lay them to dry on top of a white or colorfast towel, or use a special mesh rack across the bathtub.

10 SPEED UP THE PROCESS
Don't leave thick sweaters or blankets to dry too slowly or they can start to smell damp. Speed up the process by directing an electric fan toward the clothes but don't put it too close, and never leave unattended.

10 TIPS Using a tumble dryer

A tumble dryer gives you dry clothes at the touch of a button; you don't have to depend on the vagaries of the weather. However, it will increase your energy bills and wear out your clothes faster, so only tumble-dry when you need dry clothes fast.

1 DO CHECK THE CARE LABELS
Most clothes can go in the dryer, except for heat-sensitive fabrics such as Lycra®, certain woolens, and very delicate silks. Some fabrics should be dried on a cool setting.

✓

2 SQUEEZE OUT WET ITEMS
Extract as much water as possible from your laundry before you put it in the dryer. This will save you time and money.

✓

3 DO SHAKE OUT AS YOU LOAD
As you put items in the dryer, shake them out first, one at a time. This helps remove creases that would otherwise be set by the heat.

✓

4 RESIST OVERFILLING
Don't overfill the drum. If you do, your clothes will emerge with more creases. Check the manual for the recommended (dry) weight of fabric per load and per program.

✓

5 AVOID OVERDRYING

Items that have been in the dryer for too long will become wrinkled. If this happens, add a wet bath towel to the dryer and run it again. This is an effective but energy-greedy remedy.

6 DO CHECK FOR SMALL ITEMS

When you remove the dry load, turn the drum with your hand to check that small items such as handkerchiefs and underwear aren't still inside.

7 KEEP CHILDREN SAFE

Never allow children to play or interfere with the dryer and keep them away from it while it's in use.

8 CLEAN THE FILTER

Remove fluff from the filter (usually on the front edge of the drum) after every drying cycle or there's a risk of fire. Regularly wipe around the filter opening, too, since fluff can gather there.

9 SWITCH OFF BETWEEN USES

When the dryer's not in use, switch it off, unplug it from the socket, and make sure the door's closed. This protects from the risk of an electrical fire and stops children from tampering with the dryer (see tip 7).

10 CLEAN INSIDE AND OUT

Every few months, wipe the inside of the dryer with a cloth that's been barely dampened with warm, soapy water. Occasionally wipe the exterior with a damp cloth, too.

Ironing kit

Before you tackle a pile of wrinkled shirts, make sure you have the right equipment. That means not only a clean iron and a board that's no higher than hip-level, but also a ready supply of hangers and a pressing cloth for use on suits and delicate fabrics. A lavender-and-water spray is a useful addition.

WATER SPRAY
Fill with tap water and use to dampen overly dry items before ironing.

LAVENDER OIL
A few drops added to the water spray will make your clothes smell fresh.

IRONING BOARD COVER
Make sure you buy a well-padded, heat-resistant cover that's the correct size for your ironing board.

SOLEPLATE CLEANING WIPES
Used regularly, these ensure your iron runs smoothly over the fabric.

COTTON PRESSING CLOTHS
Use a thin pressing cloth between the iron and the fabric to prevent suit material from getting shiny.

DESCALING SOLUTION
Use every 6 months or so to get rid of mineral deposits in your iron's water tank.

STEAM IRON
Choose an iron with a large-capacity water tank so you don't have to waste time refilling it. An automatic shut-off function will prevent you from scorching your clothes.

IRONING BOARD
The bigger your ironing board, the faster you'll be able to iron, since you won't need to move the clothes around so often. Always buy a height-adjustable board.

SELECTION OF HANGERS
Hang clothes right after ironing to keep them from wrinkling. Hang delicate clothes on padded hangers and use unpadded hangers for other clothes.

10 TIPS
Speed ironing

Certain shirts and blouses have to be ironed but items like towels and underwear don't. Use these simple tips and techniques to keep your ironing to the absolute minimum and to speed up the ironing that you really can't avoid.

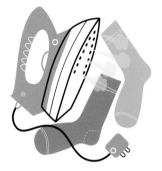

1 USE FABRIC SOFTENER
Add some fabric softener to the final rinse of your wash and your clothes will emerge from the machine with fewer wrinkles.

✔

2 TAKE ADVANTAGE OF THE DRYER
Used properly (see pp.136–7), the dryer will save you from having to iron many items. For best results, take clothes out before they're completely dry, then shake them out right away.

✔

3 FOLD BEFORE IRONING
No matter how you dry them, instead of dumping your clothes in a pile while you get around to ironing them, fold them carefully. You'll then have fewer creases to contend with.

✔

4 BUY "PERMANENT PRESS"
Man-made fibers are often labeled "permanent press." These fabrics won't need ironing but it's worth hanging items made from them in the bathroom where the steam will remove any creases.

5 KEEP IRONING TO A MINIMUM
Hang skirts and dresses to dry so you don't have to iron them, and don't bother to iron towels, underwear, or bedding.

6 IRON AT THE CORRECT TEMPERATURE
Check the care label instructions before ironing. If you set the iron to the correct temperature, you'll iron faster and you won't damage the clothes.

7 IRON FROM COOLEST TO HOTTEST
Start by ironing the clothes that need the coolest temperature and work your way up to those that need the hottest. That way you won't have to wait for the iron to cool down.

8 IRON COTTON AND LINEN
To look their best, cotton and linen clothing should always be ironed. For best results, iron while slightly damp, or dampen a little with the spray on your steam iron or with a handheld water spray.

9 IRON DISH TOWELS AND HANDKERCHIEFS
If at all possible, you should iron dish towels and handkerchiefs, if only because it helps to sterilize them.

10 AVOID IRONING DIRTY CLOTHES
Never be tempted to try and freshen up dirty clothes by ironing them. The heat from the iron can set any stains in the fabric and they'll be impossible to remove.

3 MIN Iron a collar and cuffs

There are always emergencies when, no matter how hard you try, you just can't find time to iron the shirt or blouse you need in a hurry. The only thing to do is cheat. Three minutes are all it takes to set the iron and ironing board up and iron the collar and cuffs. Keep your jacket on and no one will ever know!

→1

Lay the collar flat on the ironing board and iron the inside. Then fold the collar along the natural fold line and iron the outside, particularly along the fold.

→2

Slip one shoulder over the narrow end of the ironing board. Iron the shoulder panel toward the sleeve, then turn the shirt around and iron the other panel.

BEFORE YOU BEGIN

ADJUST THE IRONING BOARD → Make sure the board's at hip height.

ADJUST THE TEMPERATURE → Make sure the temperature's correctly set to match the fabric you're ironing and give the iron time to reach that temperature.

HAVE EVERYTHING ON HAND → You may need a water spray bottle to get rid of creases.

Extra tips

It's quicker to iron shirts when they're still a little damp. If they're too dry, dampen by spraying with the spray on your iron or with a handheld spray.

To iron gathers, place the iron with the gathers opening in the direction of the tip of the iron, then wiggle the tip into each gather in turn.

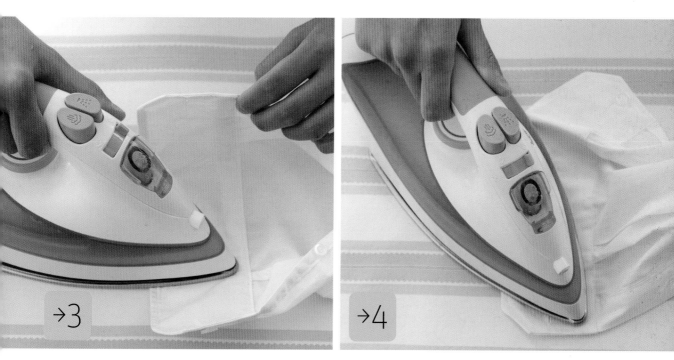

Make sure the cuffs are unbuttoned, then place one cuff on the ironing board, buttons facing down, and iron the inside using the tip of the iron.

Turn the cuff over and iron the outside. Avoid ironing any part of the sleeve and don't iron over the buttons, in case they melt. Repeat for the other cuff.

3 MIN Iron a shirt front and sleeves

There's no doubt that a shirt looks neater when it's ironed, even a shirt that's made from permanent press fabric. If you've already ironed the collar and cuffs (see pp.142–3), you only need 3 minutes more to iron the front and sleeves. With practice, you can iron the whole shirt in 5 minutes.

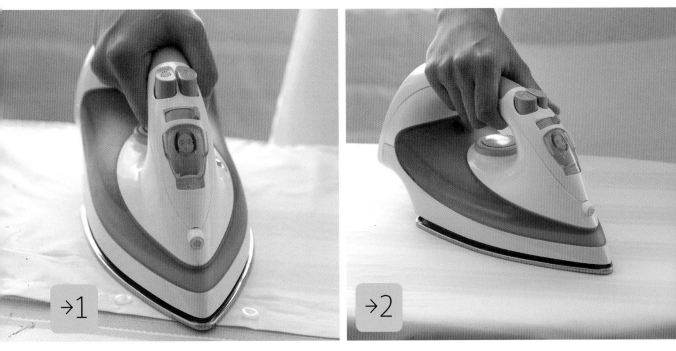

→1

Slip the shirt front, buttons facing upward, over the ironing board. Iron in between the buttons, then iron the rest of the front. Iron the other shirt front.

→2

Slip the back of the shirt over the ironing board and iron it. Revolve the shirt, smoothing it out with your hands and ironing it until you reach the other front.

Extra tips

To iron silk garments, leave them slightly damp, turn them inside out, and use the coolest setting. Don't spray any areas with water, since this will leave a mark.

To iron a sequined garment, put it face down on a thick towel, lay a pressing cloth on top, and iron over that on a cool setting.

To iron lined clothes, turn inside out to iron the lining first, then turn the right way and iron the outer fabric.

Always iron vintage clothing with care, especially if there's no care label. Hot ironing isn't a good idea. It's better to use the coolest setting and/or a pressing cloth to protect the fabric. Press, don't iron.

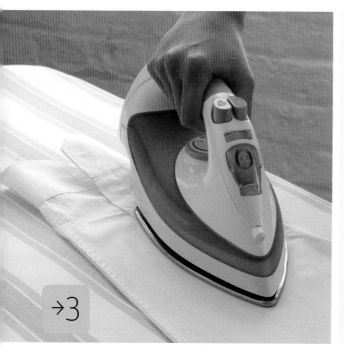

→3

Lay the sleeve along the board so its side seams are lying flat. Iron along the sleeve, moving from cuff to shoulder. Repeat for the other sleeve.

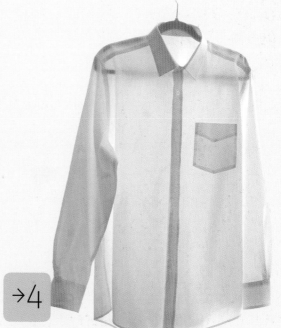

→4

Don't ruin your good work by letting the shirt become creased. Place it on a hanger and fasten the top few buttons to help the shirt keep its shape.

2 MIN Fold a shirt

There's nothing more annoying than wasting time trying to find a particular shirt, blouse, sweater, or T-shirt. Master this speedy folding technique, then you can stow your tops in a neat stack on a shelf or in a drawer. When it's time to get dressed, it only takes a moment to find the top you need.

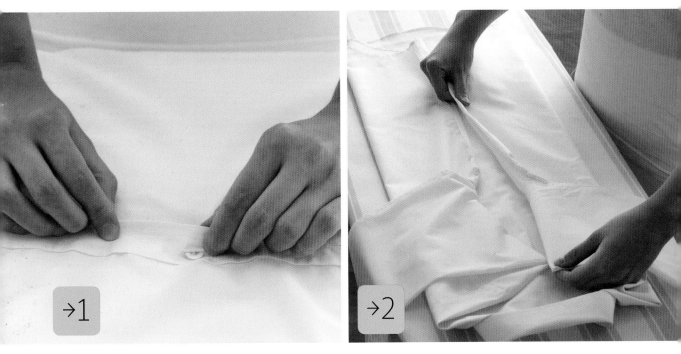

→1

With the shirt on a flat surface, button it up at the top, middle, and bottom buttons. This helps the shirt keep its shape. Don't bother to button the cuffs.

→2

Now lay the shirt face down. Leaving the sleeves hanging at either side, fold each side of the shirt inward so that the two meet down the middle of the back.

Extra tips

If the shirt has a shirttail, fold it up between steps 3 and 4 to make a straight line before you fold the rest of the shirt into thirds.

To fold tailored pants ready to hang, lay one leg on top of the other and align the front and back creases. Hang by the bottom edge or fold over a pants hanger.

For wrinkle-free packing of suits and dresses, hang in garment bags then fold the bags into your case.

To get rid of wrinkles from clothes that have been in a suitcase, unpack as soon as you arrive and hang the garments on a plastic hanger in the bathroom while you take a shower.

→3

Pick up one sleeve and lay it down the back so it's aligned with the side fold. Repeat with the other sleeve. Your shirt should now be in the shape of a rectangle.

→4

Fold up the bottom third, including the sleeves and cuffs. Then fold the top third, including the collar, back over the other two-thirds.

10 TIPS

Bed linen care

Although comforters, pillows, and blankets need cleaning, the good news is that you don't have to do it more than once or twice a year—and in between you can easily keep them fresh. If in doubt about how to clean, follow the advice on the care label.

1 SPOT-TREAT STAINS
Deal with stains on pillows, blankets, and comforters as soon as you notice them. Use handwash laundry detergent and a damp sponge, rinse, then dry in a warm place or dry with a hairdryer.

2 FRESHEN UP PILLOWS
Every month, freshen pillows by putting them in a hot dryer for 15 minutes (the heat kills dust mites) or by hanging them outside.

3 WASH PILLOWS
Every 6 months, machine-wash pillows on the gentlest cycle, unless the care label states they're not washable. Don't add fabric softener. Finish either by tumble- or line-drying.

4 FRESHEN COMFORTERS
Every 6 months, freshen comforters by tumble-drying on a hot setting. If the care label states they can't be tumble-dried, hang outdoors for a few hours.

5 WASH COMFORTERS INFREQUENTLY
Comforters only need to be washed once a year, and less frequently if they contain feathers. Only machine-wash if advised on the care label.

6 PROFESSIONALLY WASH LARGE COMFORTERS
King-size and California-king-size comforters won't fit in a domestic washing machine or dryer. You'll need to have them laundered professionally.

7 PREVENT CLUMPING IN THE DRYER
To prevent the filling in a comforter or in pillows from clumping together when tumble-dried, always add a couple of colorfast tennis balls in the dryer with the items.

8 REVIVE GRAYING SHEETS
To brighten graying bed linen, soak for 2 hours with stain-removing detergent at 3tbsp (40g) per quart (liter) hot water before putting it in the wash.

9 RESHAPE WHILE DAMP
If you have a machine-washable blanket, measure it before washing so you can reshape it to its original dimensions while it's drying.

10 DRY-CLEAN WOOLEN BLANKETS
Many woolen bedspreads and blankets have to be dry-cleaned (check the care label), although you can spot-treat stains in the same way as other bedding (see tip 1).

10 TIPS Successful dry cleaning

It may be expensive, but dry cleaning is the only way to keep some of the finest, most delicate garments in your wardrobe looking their best. If the item's precious, consider going to a specialist rather than using an express service.

1 AVOID BUYING TOO MANY DRY-CLEAN-ONLY ITEMS
To reduce the inconvenience as well as your dry cleaning bills, avoid buying clothes that are dry-clean-only. Before you buy anything new, make a habit of checking the care label first.

2 CHECK GARMENT LABELS CAREFULLY
Ignore the garment's care label at your peril. The most likely reason for recommending that an item be dry-cleaned is to prevent it from shrinking, losing its shape, or leaking dye into the wash.

3 LOOK FOR THE LETTER "P"
If an item has a care label with an letter P or F in a circle this means that it must be dry-cleaned with particular care. Point this out in case your dry cleaner isn't prepared to accept responsibility for damage.

4 KEEP MATCHING ITEMS TOGETHER
Dry-clean sets of items at the same time, in case the colors fade. For example, send suit jackets and pants or pairs of curtains to the dry cleaners together.

5 KNOW YOUR RIGHTS

Care labels are covered under consumer law in most countries, so if a dry-clean-only item has shrunk when you get it back from the cleaners, you can ask the manufacturer to repair or replace it.

6 AVOID STORING IN PLASTIC BAGS

When you get your clothes home, remove the plastic cover, as it can stain the clothes indelibly. Replace the wire hanger with a plastic, wooden, or padded one. A good hanger will extend the life of your clothes.

7 GET RID OF THE SMELL

If there's a smell of dry-cleaning solvent on your clothes when you get them back, don't hang them in your closet right away. First, let them air outside or in a well-ventilated room for a day.

8 DO NOT LEAVE STAINED ITEMS TOO LONG

If you have a stained a dry-clean-only item, don't leave it lying around for days. Take it to the dry cleaners as soon as possible, point out the stain, and say what caused it. This will help them treat it correctly.

9 AVOID WASHING DRY-CLEAN-ONLY ITEMS REPEATEDLY

If you do decide to go ahead and wash a dry-clean-only item, don't do it often. The impact of washing may only become apparent after several washes.

10 AVOID DRY CLEANING FEATHERS AND DOWN

Dry cleaning strips the natural oils from down and feathers in pillows and coats, and it's this that keeps you warm. Laundering at a low temperature is often best, but consult the care label first.

Shoe-cleaning kit

You can polish your shoes the old-fashioned way by removing surface dirt, applying wax with a shoe brush, rubbing it off with a second brush, and buffing to a shine with a dust cloth. This only takes a few minutes, but if you prefer, you can use an even faster self-shining product. Specialized products include cleaners for suede and nubuck, as well as waterproofing products.

PAPER TOWEL
Use to apply baby oil and also to pack into wet shoes to absorb the moisture.

SHOE BRUSHES
Use one to apply polish and another for rubbing the polish off. Keep a pair for each color.

DUST CLOTHS
Use to buff shoes to a shine. Keep one for each color polish.

BAKING SODA
Sprinkle in shoes to remove odor overnight.

BABY OIL
Use a spot on a sheet of paper towel to restore the shine to patent leather.

WATERPROOFING SPRAY
Use on new shoes before you wear them and reapply to clean shoes from time to time.

SUEDE CLEANER
Specially formulated for suede and nubuck, these cleaners often incorporate a plastic brush in the cap.

MICROFIBER CLOTH
This works just as well as a dust cloth to buff shoes and is less likely to leave fluff behind.

SELF-SHINING POLISH
Just a wipe makes shoes look like new, but it doesn't feed the leather like traditional polish.

RUBBER GLOVES
To protect your hands when cleaning shoes.

TRADITIONAL SHOE POLISH
Use to nourish the leather and stop it from drying out and cracking.

NEWSPAPER
In the interest of hygiene, use some newspaper to protect surfaces when you're polishing shoes.

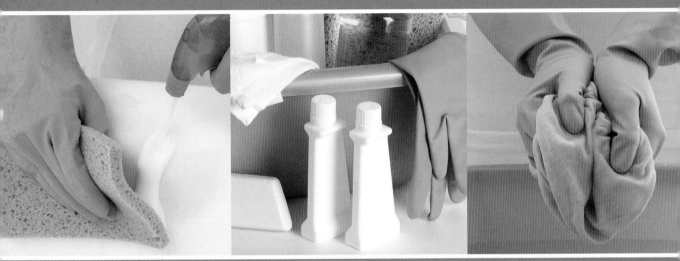

Removing stains

Stain-removal kit

The secret to successful stain removal is to act quickly and to blot up spills with paper towels as soon as they happen. Always work from the outside edge of the stain toward the center and dab, don't scrub. For tough stains, start with the mildest remedy and work up to the knockout chemical attack.

CARPET-CLEANING SPRAY
Use to remove red wine and urine stains from carpets.

METHYLATED SPIRITS
Use for removing tough grass stains and felt-tip pen marks.

TALCUM POWDER
Useful for removing greasy stains.

DETERGENT WITH OXYGEN BLEACH
Containing hydrogen peroxide (see opposite), it is gentler than household bleach and suits many fabrics.

CLEAN WHITE CLOTHS
Use to absorb stains. Avoid colored cloths in case the dye transfers to the item you're cleaning.

WASH TUB
Put clothes in to soak.

STAIN-REMOVAL BAR
Use before you wash for dealing with stains on clothes. See also p.130.

STAIN-REMOVAL LIQUID
Keep this in your armory of spot-cleaning products. See also p.130.

PAPER TOWEL
Use this as quickly as possible to blot up spills and so prevent stains.

SODA WATER
Encourages spills like red wine and urine to bubble to the surface so you can blot them up.

SPONGE
Use to dab at stains, working from the outside in.

RUBBER GLOVES
To protect your hands while you're working with stain removers.

HYDROGEN PEROXIDE
A last resort for removing otherwise stubborn old sweat stains.

BRANDED STAIN REMOVERS
Keep a selection in your kit to remove specific types of stain.

Remove a red wine stain from a carpet

5 MIN

Red wine, unlike white, is renowned for staining. But act swiftly and you won't have a problem. The sooner you splash on some soda water, the greater your chances of getting rid of the stain completely.

BARE ESSENTIALS

paper towels

soda water

sponges

aerosol carpet cleaner

vacuum cleaner

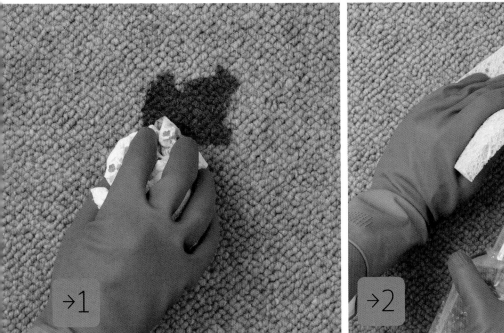

→1 **Use paper towels** to absorb as much wine as possible. Blot from the outside of the stain toward the center to prevent the stain from spreading.

→2 **Splash a little soda water** onto the stain to encourage the wine to bubble up to the surface. Then blot it with a sponge, taking care not to rub. Repeat if necessary.

BEFORE YOU BEGIN

PUT ON RUBBER GLOVES → These will protect your hands from the carpet cleaner, which may contain toxic ingredients.

CLEAR THE AREA → Move furniture and make sure rugs are folded out of the way.

KEEP PETS AND CHILDREN AWAY → They must not come into contact with the carpet cleaner, as it may contain toxic ingredients.

Extra tips

Don't believe the one about covering a red-wine stain with salt. It simply sets the stain.

To remove red wine from clothing and upholstery, sponge with lukewarm water, blot to remove excess, then use a proprietary stain remover designed for wine and fruit-juice stains.

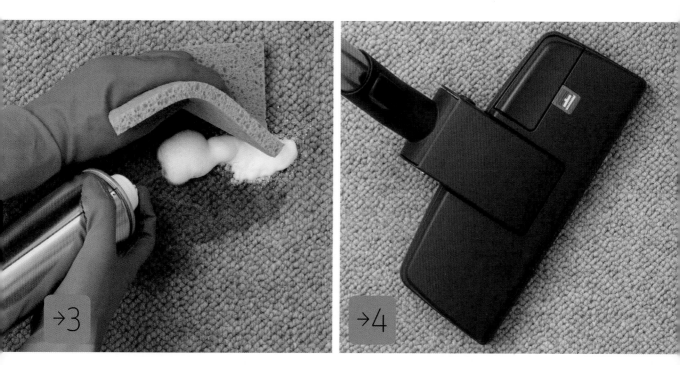

→3

Thoroughly shake the can of aerosol carpet cleaner, then spray it onto the affected area. Work the foam in gently using a clean, damp sponge.

→4

Leave until the carpet is completely dry, then vacuum the affected area. If the stain remains, repeat the process, this time starting from step 3.

Remove ink stains from a sofa

3 MIN

Don't panic if you discover that your favorite sofa has been used as a drawing board. Many inks today are washable and will come out easily. This simple method works for both felt-tip and ballpoint inks.

BARE ESSENTIALS

paper towels

upholstery cleaning spray

sponge

colorfast towel

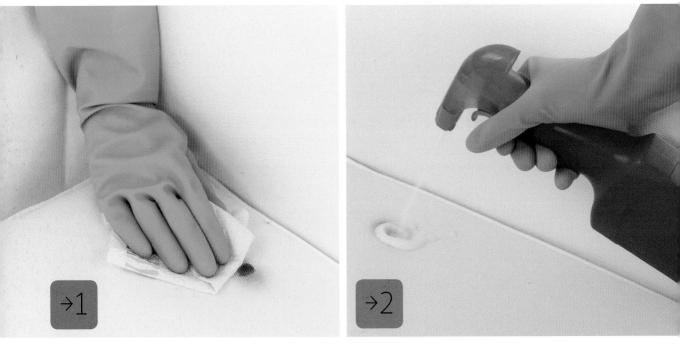

→1

→2

As soon as you can, blot the stained area with a piece of paper towel to remove any excess ink. Blot from the outside to the inside to keep from spreading the stain.

Following the manufacturer's instructions, spray a little upholstery cleaner on the stain, then leave the product to work for the recommended time.

Extra tips

Remove ink stains from washable clothing by using an oxygen-bleach detergent, a branded stain remover for ink stains (follow the manufacturer's instructions), or by dabbing with methylated spirit (test first for colorfastness on an inconspicuous part of the garment), followed by rinsing and washing.

Remove ballpoint ink from clothing by using a solvent such as dry-cleaning fluid, lighter fuel, or methylated spirit, or by dabbing with rubbing alcohol or vodka. Test first for colorfastness. After use, rinse in cold water, then wash as normal.

Don't wash ink-stained clothing until you have removed as much stain as you can or the stain will set.

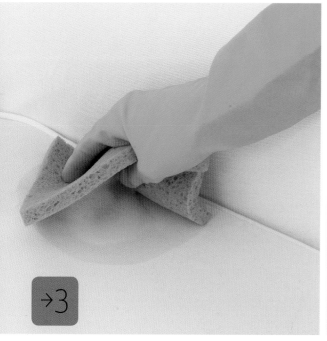

→3

Blot the area with a clean damp sponge, being careful not to spread the stain. If the stain remains, reapply the upholstery cleaner and leave to work as before.

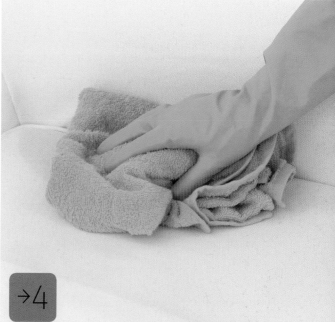

→4

Finish by removing excess moisture from the area. Place an old, colorfast towel on top to absorb the moisture and leave until the area's almost dry, then let air-dry.

Remove grass stains from clothing

5 MIN

Light grass stains may come out in the wash without a prewash soaking but to be sure, you'll need to use a stain-removing product, especially if the clothing is white or light-colored.

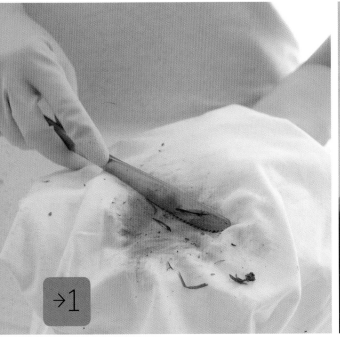

→1

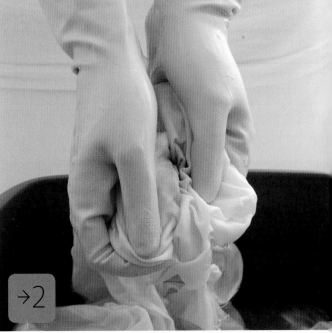

→2

Working as quickly as possible, start by scraping away any loose pieces of grass from the surface of the fabric using a blunt knife. Go carefully, to keep from damaging the fabric.

Immerse the stained area in a tub filled with cold water. Leave to soak for a few minutes, then rub fabric against fabric to break up the stain.

ACTION PLAN

BEFORE YOU START → Put on rubber gloves to protect your hands from drying out.

AS YOU WORK → Make sure you soak the clothing in cold water, since grass is a protein and hot water will set the stain.

AFTERWARD → Follow the correct washing and drying instructions for the fabric.

Extra tips

To remove old grass stains, dab with a 1:4 solution of methylated spirit and water, rinse in warm soapy water, then launder or dry clean.

To remove grass stains from delicates, apply the stain remover using a cloth with a gentle circular movement, then handwash.

Apply a stain-removal stick and again rub fabric against fabric. If the stain still persists, rinse, apply more stain remover, and rub again.

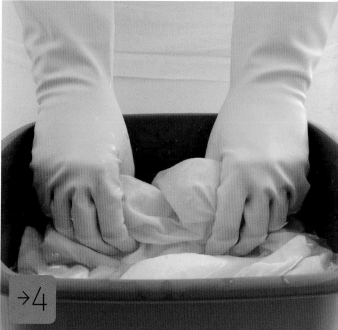

Finish by rinsing in plenty of clean water, then launder the item at the highest possible temperature recommended on the care label.

Remove grease stains from clothing

5 MIN

Tackling grease stains requires a fast, two-pronged attack. First, remove excess grease by dry-blotting and then move onto using water and detergent. If the stain's old, take the garment to the dry cleaner.

BARE ESSENTIALS

paper towels

sponge

handwash laundry detergent

wash tub

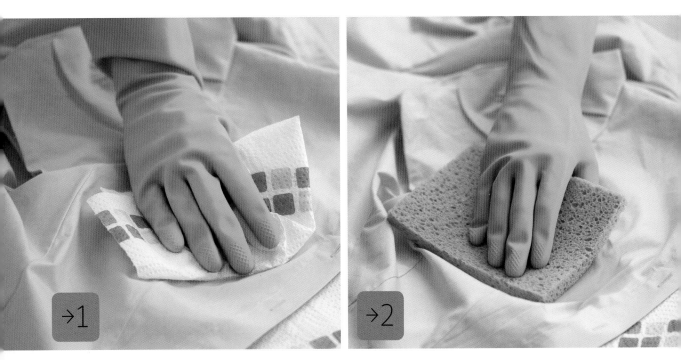

→1

As soon as you can, lay the stained area on a piece of paper towel to help absorb the grease. Blot the other side of the fabric with another piece of paper towel.

→2

Repeat, using clean pieces of paper towel until the worst of the grease has been absorbed, then dampen the area using a sponge and cold water.

Extra tips

Removing grease from upholstery, requires a similar approach to removing it from clothing. Blot up as much grease as possible using paper towels, then sprinkle with talcum powder, Fuller's earth, or cornstarch. Leave to absorb the grease, then vacuum off using the dusting-brush attachment. If the stain persists, follow steps 3–4 on p.173.

Remove grease from a carpet by blotting with a piece of paper towel, then using dry-cleaning fluid. Or use a dry-stick spot cleaner to absorb the grease, leave for a few minutes, then brush or vacuum away.

Remove grease from wallpaper using dry-cleaning fluid. Test for colorfastness on an inconspicuous part of the paper first.

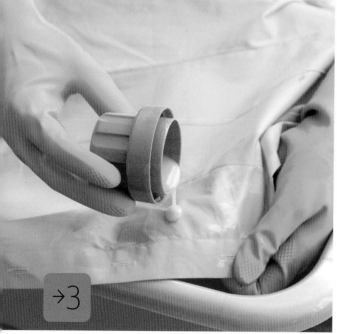

→3

Put a little handwash laundry detergent on the stain and work it in. Don't rub or the stain might spread. Soak at the highest temperature recommended for the fabric.

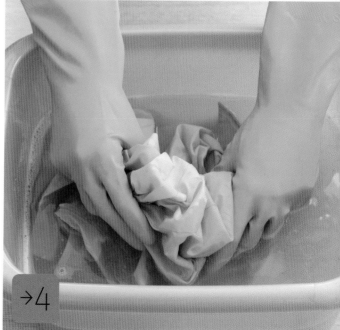

→4

Soak for 30 minutes. If the stain persists, add some handwash detergent and soak again. Finally, wash at the highest possible temperature or handwash, if required.

Remove perspiration stains from clothing

3 MIN

Don't leave sweaty clothes sitting in the laundry basket or the stains will be more difficult to remove. Today's oxygen-bleach detergents work well on a wide range of fabrics and speed up stain removal.

→1

→2

Take the item of clothing off as soon as possible. Fill a wash tub with warm water, add the clothing, and let it soak for 10 minutes. This loosens the stain.

Remove the clothing, refill the tub with clean, warm water, and then add the recommended amount of oxygen-bleach detergent.

Extra tips

If you notice unsightly white deodorant marks on your clothes, there's no need to change. Try rubbing the area with a pair of pantyhose or with a dark sock.

To remove perspiration stains the traditional way, sponge with a solution of 1tbsp (15ml) white vinegar to 1 cup (250ml) warm water, then rinse and wash as normal. If the garment can't be washed, sponge with the vinegar solution (test first for colorfastness), then dry-clean.

To remove old perspiration stains from washable fabric, soften the stain first by dabbing with a little glycerin. Alternatively, if the fabric is white, pour a little hydrogen peroxide on the stained area, rub it in gently, leave for 5 minutes, then wash as normal.

→3

Dissolve the oxygen-bleach detergent completely, then immerse the clothing in the solution. Gently rub fabric against fabric in the area of the stain.

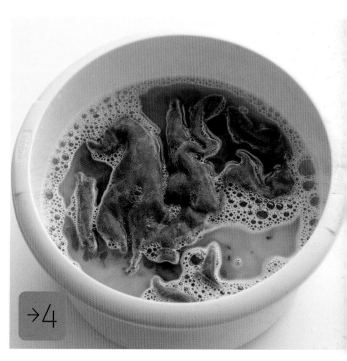

→4

Leave to soak for another 30 minutes, then rinse in cold water. Once the stain has gone, launder at the hottest temperature recommended on the care label.

Remove urine stains from a carpet

10 MIN

Urine can remove dye and may damage wool and nylon, so eliminate it from carpets and fabrics as quickly as you can. The smell of cat urine lingers, too, so use a deodorizing spray after step 4.

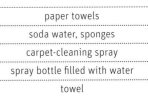

BARE ESSENTIALS

paper towels

soda water, sponges

carpet-cleaning spray

spray bottle filled with water

towel

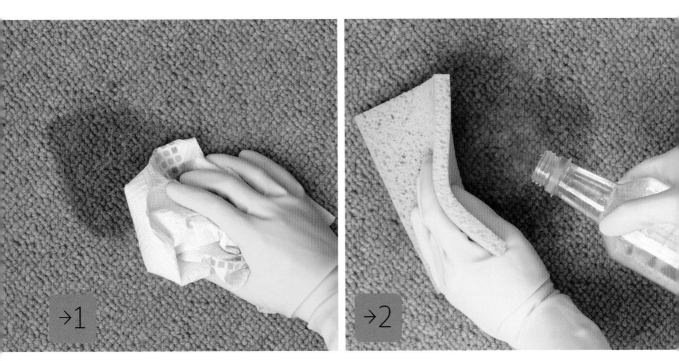

→1

Blot up the urine as soon as possible using paper towels. Use fresh pieces of paper towel and keep blotting until the paper towel comes away dry.

→2

Pour a little soda water onto the stain to bring the urine to the surface, then soak up the moisture with a dry sponge or with more paper towels.

ACTION PLAN

BEFORE YOU START → Put on rubber gloves for hygiene reasons.

CLEAR THE AREA → Move furniture and make sure rugs are folded out of the way.

AFTERWARD → If you need to speed up the drying process, you can use a hairdryer on a cool setting after step 4.

Extra tips

To remove dried-on urine, dampen the stain with a sponge, then continue from step 2.

To remove urine from clothes, soak overnight in warm water with a little biological detergent (detergent with enzymes for breaking down proteins), then wash and dry in the usual way.

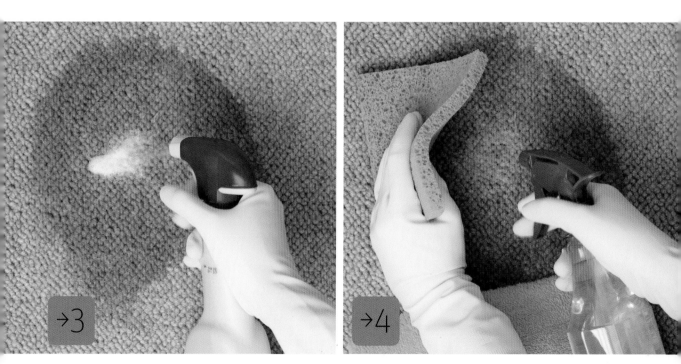

→3

Spray the stained area with a carpet-cleaning product, then work the product gently into the stain from the outside in, using a damp sponge.

→4

Using a clean sponge and a spray bottle of water, rinse the area. Take care not to get the carpet too wet. Finish by using an old towel to soak up any moisture.

Remove blood stains from clothing

As with all stains, the longer blood sits on a fabric, the tougher it is to remove. These instructions work for stains a day old or less. If they're older, you may need to repeat steps 2–4. And because blood's a protein, only use cold water on it, or the stain will set.

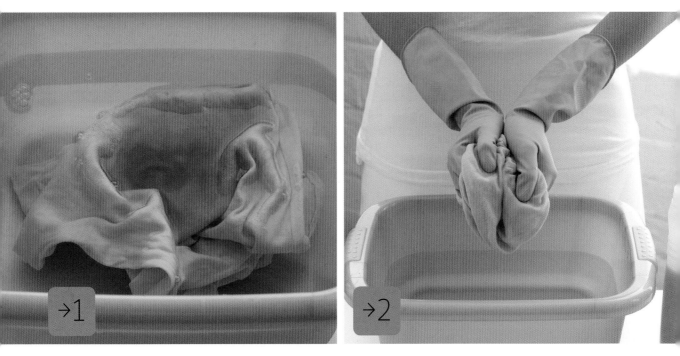

→1

Remove the item of clothing as soon as possible and immerse it in a wash tub filled with cold water. This will help to loosen the blood.

→2

Rub a little handwash laundry detergent into the remaining stain. Rub the area firmly between your fists, with your palms facing each other.

ACTION PLAN

BEFORE YOU START → If the blood is fresh, rinse the clothing under cold water to flush away excess blood before starting step 1.

AS YOU WORK → Be sure to soak the clothing in cold water, since hot water will set the stain.

AFTERWARD → Make sure the stain has been removed before ironing, or the heat of the iron will set the stain.

Extra tips

To remove blood stains from delicates, apply the handwash laundry detergent with a sponge, using a gentle circular movement. Rinse, then dry.

To remove blood stains from upholstery, blot with paper towels, dab with water and a little handwash laundry detergent, spray with water, then blot dry.

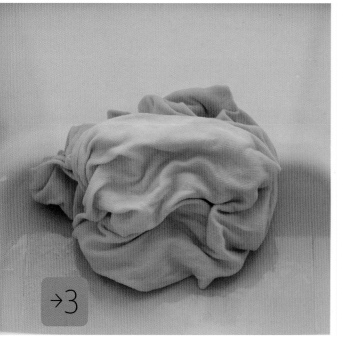

→3

Leave the wet clothing for 15 minutes for the detergent to work. If you're treating several garments, be careful not to let the damp articles touch or the colors may run.

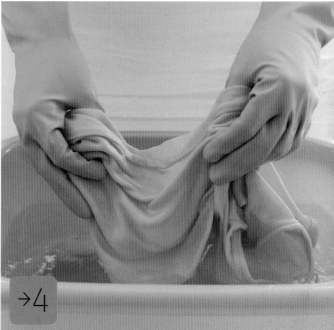

→4

If the stain's gone completely, rinse thoroughly and hang to dry. If there's still some residual stain, wash the item according to the care label.

Remove food stains from upholstery

4 MIN

Stains from food are common on upholstery but can usually be removed in a matter of minutes. Follow the simple steps below to remove non-liquid stains such as jam or chocolate.

BARE ESSENTIALS

knife, paper towels, plastic bowl

handwash laundry detergent, sponges

upholstery cleaning spray

spray bottle filled with water, colorfast towel

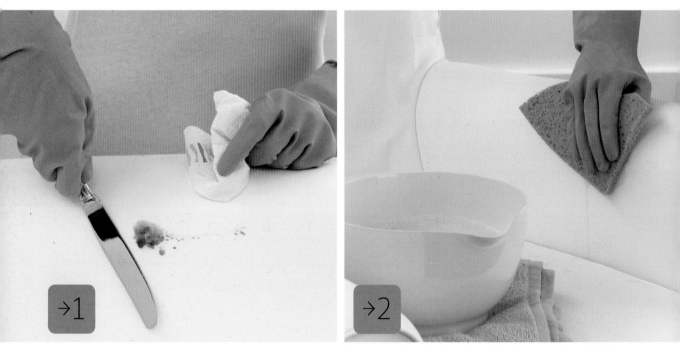

→1

→2

Start by scraping off any excess food using the blunt edge of a knife. Take care not to spread the food, so be sure to wipe the knife clean on paper towels as you work.

Follow the manufacturer's instructions to make a solution of handwash laundry detergent and cool water. Sponge on gently without rubbing to avoid spreading the stain.

Extra tips

To remove coffee stains from upholstery, blot the excess liquid using a piece of paper towel, then pour on a little soda water and blot with a clean piece of paper towel. Repeat until the stain has gone or, if you can't remove it all by this method, continue with steps 3–4 below.

To remove a tea stain from upholstery, blot the stain to remove the excess tea using a piece of paper towel, then spray on some cold water and blot with a clean piece of paper towel. If this doesn't work, try dabbing with a solution of biological detergent and water, then rinse this out with a spray of cold water. Blot dry with a colorfast towel, then let air-dry.

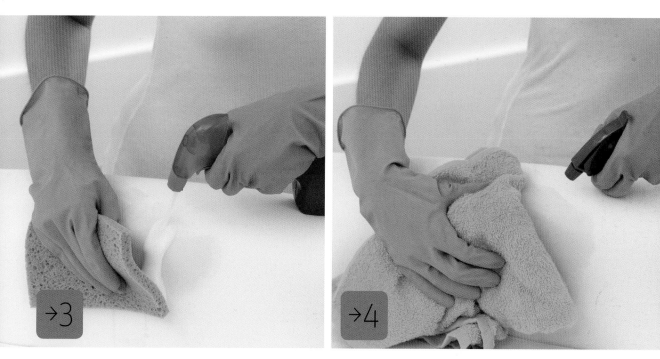

If the stain persists, spray a little upholstery cleaner on the stain. Blot with a clean damp sponge, being careful not to spread the stain.

Using a spray bottle filled with tap water, moisten—don't soak—the stained area, then blot it with a colorfast towel. When it's almost dry, let it air-dry.

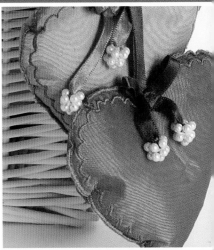

Coping with
children and pets

10 TIPS Successful delegation

Family housework doesn't have to be done by just one person. You need help, especially if you do a paid job, too. Encourage everyone in the house to feel part of the cleaning team and if you find you're still struggling, it may be time to employ a cleaner.

1 START THEM YOUNG
Even toddlers can start to help their parents by putting away their toys, placing dirty clothes in a laundry basket, and carrying things to and from the table.

2 SAY WHAT YOU EXPECT
Once children are 10 or older, you can expect them to make their own beds, sort their dirty laundry, vacuum their room, help with dishes, and load and empty the dishwasher.

3 GET CHILDREN'S HELP AT MEALTIMES
If children are hanging around waiting for a meal, involve them in preparations by asking them to clear and set the table. Make sure they make an effort to put their own dishes away, too.

4 GIVE CHILDREN CHOICES
To encourage children to help with chores, give them a choice. Ask if they'd like to empty the dishwasher or clear up the coffee table. They'll be happier to perform a task if it's one they've chosen themselves.

5 GIVE PARTNERS CHOICES

Giving a choice can also work with partners. Explain what needs to be done around the house one evening and ask your partner which of the tasks they'd like to do.

6 PRAISE GENEROUSLY

Even if the job isn't done as well as you might do it, don't criticize. You can point out what needs to be done to complete the job, but remember to praise what has been done.

7 EXPLAIN WHY

Children will be more likely to help if they understand the purpose of cleaning up. Explain that it will give them more space to play, make things easier to find, and prevent their toys from getting stepped on and broken.

8 RESIST SUPERVISING OLDER CHILDREN

Resist the urge to supervise older children when they're cleaning. Let them take responsibility for a task and they'll feel more satisfied when it's completed.

9 HELP THE CLEANER ON THE FIRST DAY

The first day your cleaner comes, make sure you're there to oversee things. Have a list of jobs you'd like to have done so you can help your cleaner to establish a routine.

10 TELL THE CLEANER WHAT TO USE

Point out the materials you'd like your cleaner to use, or you may find bleach used everywhere or bathroom sponges being used for washing the dishes.

Child's bedroom speed-clean

15 MIN

Although children can help around the house from a young age, when it comes to transforming their bedrooms from chaos to calm sanctuary, chances are you'll have to take the lead. In 15 minutes, you should be able to straighten up a messy bedroom.

1 BRING IN THE FRESH AIR
Open the window to let in some fresh air while you clean. It will also reduce humidity and warmth, which will help prevent dust mites.

2 MAKE THE BED
Shake out the bedding and leave it to air while you do the rest of the jobs. Before you leave the room, make up the bed, plumping the pillows and smoothing out the comforter or blankets.

3 CLEAR UP MESSY THINGS
If your child has been painting, coloring, or doing other messy activities, put everything away. If the child's around, get him or her to lend a hand to encourage them to help in the future.

4 CHECK FOR STAINS
Check the carpet and upholstery for spills or stains. Deal immediately with any that you find, using the appropriate detergent and stain-removal method.

5 PICK UP CLOTHES

Pick up any clothes from the floor and give them a firm shake to remove dust and dirt. Then hang them in the closet or fold them and put them away in drawers.

✓

6 CHECK FOR DIRTY CLOTHES

Ideally, your child will have a laundry basket in the room, so if you come across dirty clothes, put them in. Alternatively, make a pile near the door to take to the laundry hamper when you leave the room.

✓

7 DEAL WITH THE TOYS

Pick up toys and replace in toy-storage containers. If you come across any that are grubby, wipe them with a damp sponge. If they can be machine-washed, add them to the laundry pile.

✓

8 DAMP-DUST

Using a damp microfiber cloth, quickly wipe bedside tables and other surfaces to remove dust. If lampshades are dusty, make sure they're unplugged, then wipe them with a barely damp cloth.

✓

9 EMPTY THE WASTE-PAPER BASKET

Empty the waste-paper basket, separating any items that can be recycled and putting the rest with the household garbage. Line with a trash bag.

✓

10 FINISH BY VACUUMING

Focus on the most-used areas like the doorway and alongside the bed. Use the crevice nozzle in the corners. If there's time, pull out the bed and vacuum behind.

✓

Child's room storage

Toys, books, clothes, crayons, notebooks, and teddy bears—you'll find all this and more in a child's bedroom. Clever and attractive storage is the key to keeping it all neat. Choose multipurpose items wherever possible, make use of the end of the bed, under the bed, and of shelves, and store everything where the child can reach it. And of course, as soon as she's old enough, encourage her to keep her own room neat.

TOY CADDY
Toys your child might want while she's in bed can be stored in a toy caddy that buttons over the side of the bed.

TOY TRUNK
Keep toys that are used less often or spare bedding in a decorative toy trunk.

UNDER-BED STORAGE
Use baskets or fabric organizers to store small, often-used toys under the bed. This is the ideal location for small children's toys, since they can easily reach their playthings. In an older child's room, choose boxes with lids

PENCIL HOLDER
Put pens and pencils in a pretty plastic cup to keep them all in one place instead of scattered around the room.

BOOKCASE
Choose a bookcase with cubbyholes or a modular unit if you want to store a variety of items instead of just books.

MAGAZINE FILE
Use to store magazines and comic books and keep them all in one place. There are plenty of decorative versions around that don't immediately shout "office."

STUFFED TOYS
Get your child to put her stuffed toys "to bed" in their storage basket. It will encourage her to go to bed, too. And make sure that all stuffed toys can be washed easily.

BOX FILES
Encourage older children to file their homework in decorative box files. That way it will stay clean and free of creases.

CUSHION
Use a cushion on top of a trunk to provide extra seating.

STORAGE BASKETS
Have a variety of sizes and label them—with a picture of the contents if you like, to encourage your child to put her things away in them.

Remove pet hair from upholstery

3 MIN

Pet hair on soft furnishings not only looks unsightly, but it also provides food for dust mites. Remove pet hair daily—especially if there are people with allergies in the home—using this quick and easy technique.

BARE ESSENTIALS

rubber glove
vacuum cleaner
dusting-brush attachment

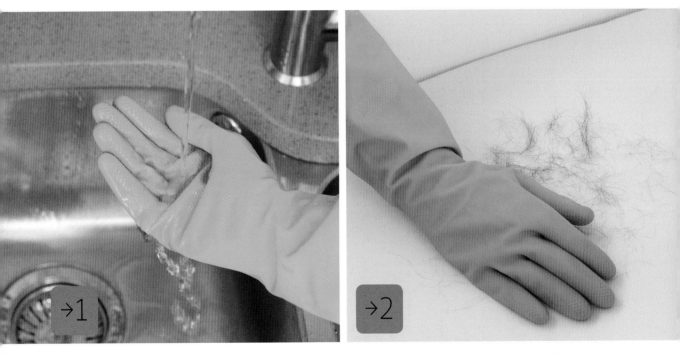

→1

Put on a rubber glove and then dampen it (and ensure it is free of detergent) by holding your gloved hand under cold, running water.

→2

With your damp, gloved hand, palm facing down, use a firm brushing motion to rub the upholstery gently. Focus on the areas with the pet hair.

Extra tips

The best way to remove pet hair from a carpet is to vacuum it. If there are any particularly densely covered areas, pick up the worst of the hair using a damp rubber glove, as below, then vacuum. Clumps of animal hair can block a vacuum cleaner.

Your first line of attack against dust mites and dander (tiny particles of an animal's dried hair or skin that dust mites thrive on) is your vacuum cleaner. Use it regularly around the home and make sure it has a HEPA filter (see pp.21 and 186).

Your second line of attack is to groom your pets regularly and do all you can to prevent them from developing dry, flaky skin (see p.187).

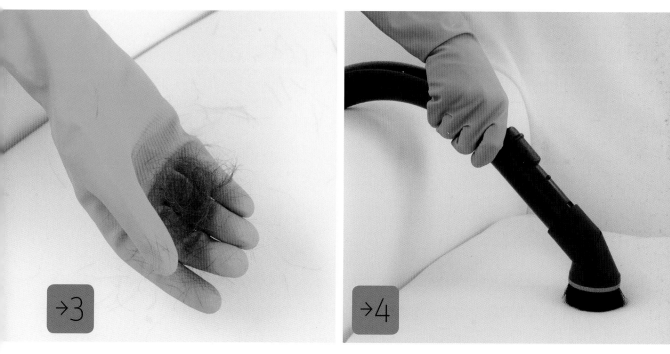

→3

Scoop up the small ball of hair that will have stuck to the damp glove, and throw it away. You may need to rinse and dampen the rubber glove again and repeat.

→4

Vacuum the upholstery using the dusting-brush attachment to pick up any remaining hair. Ideally, use a vacuum cleaner with a HEPA filter (see pp.21 and 186).

Pet-zone kit

However much we love our fluffy companions, there's no doubt they create extra work. In addition to scattering hair everywhere, pets also carry bacteria that can be dangerous to humans. Be sure you have the right kit for caring for and cleaning up after your pets, and clean up as quickly as you can. You must also tackle your general household cleaning very thoroughly.

PET BLANKET
If your cat or dog likes a certain chair, use a machine-washable blanket to cover it.

PET BASKET
Choose a design that's easy to clean.

PET BRUSH
Use to groom your cat or dog, but regularly clean the hair from the bristles.

MACHINE-WASHABLE PET BOWLS
Choose dishwasher-safe pet bowls and wash them regularly.

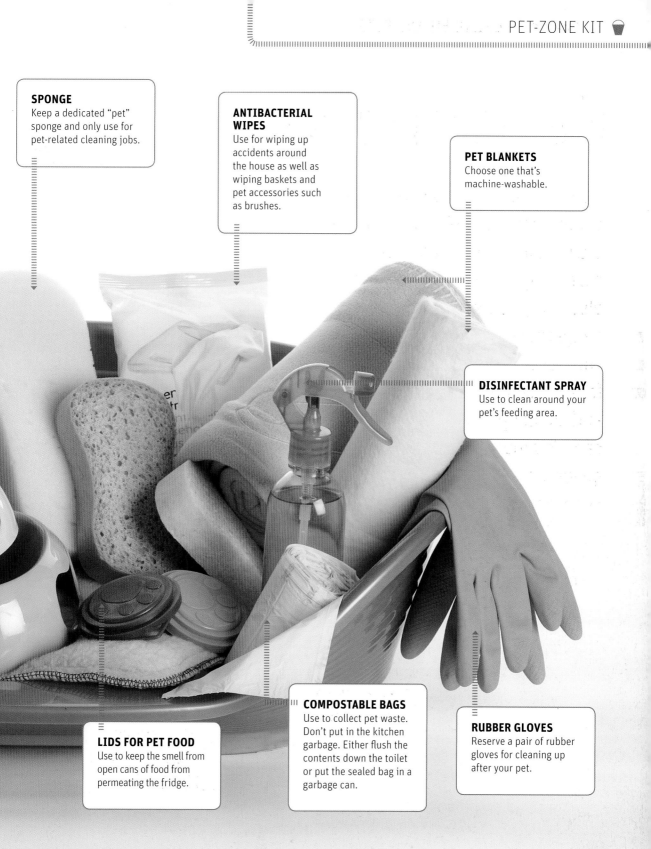

SPONGE
Keep a dedicated "pet" sponge and only use for pet-related cleaning jobs.

ANTIBACTERIAL WIPES
Use for wiping up accidents around the house as well as wiping baskets and pet accessories such as brushes.

PET BLANKETS
Choose one that's machine-washable.

DISINFECTANT SPRAY
Use to clean around your pet's feeding area.

LIDS FOR PET FOOD
Use to keep the smell from open cans of food from permeating the fridge.

COMPOSTABLE BAGS
Use to collect pet waste. Don't put in the kitchen garbage. Either flush the contents down the toilet or put the sealed bag in a garbage can.

RUBBER GLOVES
Reserve a pair of rubber gloves for cleaning up after your pet.

10 TIPS Dealing with allergies

For anyone with allergies, the main goal of housework should be to reduce dust and get rid of dust mites. Most importantly, vacuum regularly, choose the right flooring, and keep your pets out of the bedroom.

1 GET THE RIGHT VACUUM CLEANER
Make sure you have a vacuum cleaner with a HEPA (high-efficiency particulate air) filter. Dust and vacuum the house at least once a week, prioritizing the rooms you spend the most time in.

2 CHOOSE SOFT FURNISHINGS WITH CARE
Dust mites, pet hair, and dander cling to carpets, so opt for bare floors with washable rugs. Curtains also attract dust mites, so vacuum and wash them regularly. Leather sofas are better than fabric ones.

3 BUY ALLERGEN-PROOF BEDDING COVERS
Buy allergen-proof covers for pillows, mattresses, and comforters. These are tightly woven to seal out allergens from your bedding, but they're still soft and comfortable to sleep on.

4 WASH BEDDING AT A HIGH TEMPERATURE
Wash sheets, pillowcases, mattress covers, and blankets at 140°F (60°C) to kill dust mites. If the care label recommends a cool wash, placing items in the freezer for 6 hours will also kill them.

5 KEEP THINGS COOL AND DRY

Dust mites love warmth and moisture, so open windows, keep the temperature down, and use a dehumidifier, if necessary. This is particularly important in the bedroom, where mites and allergens thrive.

6 CHOOSE PET BEDDING WITH CARE

Choose pet bedding that can be machine-washed and wash it at least every two weeks. Choose wipe-clean plastic pet baskets.

7 BATHE PETS REGULARLY

Although cats hate them, regular baths reduce the amount of allergens that are spread around the home. If you start a monthly bath routine when a cat or dog is a small kitten or puppy, they may get used to it.

8 AVOID DRY, FLAKY SKIN

To prevent a dog's skin from becoming dry and flaky, add a tiny amount of vegetable oil to its diet each day—a couple of drops for a small dog and up to 1 tsp for a larger one. Give cats fish oil or sardines every week.

9 GROOM OFTEN

Make it a habit to groom your pet at least once a week. Do this job outdoors, and have the least allergic person in your family do it.

10 KEEP PETS OUT OF THE BEDROOM

Don't allow pets in bedrooms or on beds. Keep them out by shutting the bedroom doors. Wherever possible, you should also keep them off soft furnishings.

Room-freshening kit

Fresh air gets rid of most smells, so your first line of attack should be to air your home as often as possible. Also use an extractor fan or open the window while you cook, and shut the kitchen door so smells don't permeate everywhere. Before you turn to chemical air-freshening products, try a natural remedy. For instance, you can remove kitchen smells by simmering a pan of water with cloves and orange peel.

SPRAY BOTTLE
Use to scent the air with a drop or two of your favorite essential oil mixed with water.

SCENTED CANDLES
The more expensive ones are better, since the perfumes used are more likely to be natural.

CLOVE-STUDDED ORANGE
Leave this easy-to-make traditional remedy in a bowl to scent a room.

ESSENTIAL OILS
Use your favorites in a water spray or a burner. Good ones to try are lavender, rose, geranium, and orange.

HOUSEPLANTS
Peace lilies
(Spathiphyllum wallisii),
spider plants
(Chlorophytum
comosum), and palms
such as Chamaedorea
elegans are all easy to
grow and do a good job
of absorbing pollutants
in the air.

LAVENDER BAGS
Use for freshening
drawers and cupboards.

Decluttering

10 TIPS Successful decluttering

The goal of decluttering is to get rid of things you don't use and make the most of those you do.
To give yourself an incentive to declutter, imagine everything you'll be able to do with the extra space once you've decluttered a closet or entire room.

1 HAVE BAGS AND BOXES READY
Arm yourself with garbage bags for collecting broken items or things that are obviously trash, bags for items you're donating to charity or giving to friends, and storage boxes for the things you end up keeping.

2 LABEL THINGS
When you store things away in boxes, make sure you label them with sticky labels and markers. It's easy to think you'll never forget what's inside a box, but the fact is, you probably will.

3 CLEAN AS YOU GO
Take the opportunity to wipe empty drawers and cupboards clean while you're decluttering. You may wish to line clothes drawers with scented paper.

4 BE TOUGH
Try to balance the sentimental value of an object with practical concerns such as how much storage space you have and how useful the item really is.

5 ASK YOURSELF THE MAGIC QUESTIONS

The questions to ask are these: Does the item work? Do you use it? Will you remember where it is? If the answer to any of these is "no," you need to recycle the item, store it elsewhere, or throw it out.

6 RE-GIFT

Unused gifts can make fabulous presents for someone else. Use a sticky note to mark who the gift came from so you don't give it back to the person who gave it to you.

7 ONE IN, ONE OUT

For every new item you bring into your home, try to find one that you can recycle or dispose of.

8 THROW AWAY AS A LAST RESORT

Only when you've failed to sell an item, donate it to charity, recycle it, or reuse it, can you justify sending it to a landfill.

9 SET LIMITS

Don't try to reorganize your entire home all at once or you'll end up giving up in defeat. Instead, tackle one room at a time and set a time limit for the session.

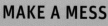

10 MAKE A MESS

Don't be scared to make things look worse first. It's impossible to do a good job of decluttering without making a mess. Only by making a mess can you then restore order.

10 TIPS Efficient recycling

Landfills are filling up fast, so we should do our best not to add to them. Luckily, you can recycle almost anything—and sometimes earn money at the same time. So when you're decluttering your home, keep in mind the following recycling tips.

1 KEEP A CHARITY BOX

Keep a box at home to store clothes, shoes, and other household items you decide you don't want. Then, every so often you can offer things to friends or family, or donate them to charity.

2 MAKE MONEY

There are many ways of turning your unwanted items into cash. Sell them via an online site such as eBay or on sites where postings are free, or make a few dollars by selling them in a garage sale.

3 GET RID OF LARGE APPLIANCES

If your old refrigerator, freezer, washing machine, dryer, or microwave is still in good working order, a charity may accept it to offer to a needy family. Otherwise, see if a local recycling center will accept it.

4 DONATE FURNITURE

Plenty of charities will collect furniture that you've grown tired of. Alternatively, post on the Freecycle™ online message board, which enables you to offer furniture and other items you don't want.

5 RECYCLE ELECTRONIC EQUIPMENT
Cell phones, MP3 players, and computers can be recycled. In some cases, computers can be overhauled for reuse. Check online for recycling centers or contact the manufacturer to find out if it has a recycling program.

6 DONATE BEDDING AND BLANKETS
Don't throw out old bedding and blankets. Instead, wash them and donate to a homeless shelter or charity. Vets and animal shelters also need supplies of towels, sheets, and blankets.

7 RECYCLE CDS AND DVDS
If you can't find a school or charity that will have your unwanted CDs and DVDs, look online to find companies that can recycle them and their packaging in an environmentally friendly way.

8 SWAP BOOKS
If you want to offload some books and replace them for free, look for book-swapping websites. You submit the books you want to get rid of and you get access to an online library to choose your replacements.

9 REDUCE
"Reduce, Reuse, Recycle" is the green mantra. The first step is to reduce. This means buying less in the first place. And when you do buy, choose the best quality you can afford so that your item lasts longer.

10 CLOSE THE LOOP
Buying products made from recycled items is just as important as recycling because it creates a demand. Try to buy as many household products and as much clothing made from recycled materials as you can.

Organize audio-visual equipment

15 MIN

Wherever there's audio-visual equipment, there's clutter. To keep from wasting time looking for a specific item—or worse, tripping over it—invest in some storage. That way, things will always be on hand.

BARE ESSENTIALS

remote-control caddy

cable organizer

CD and DVD storage unit

gaming station

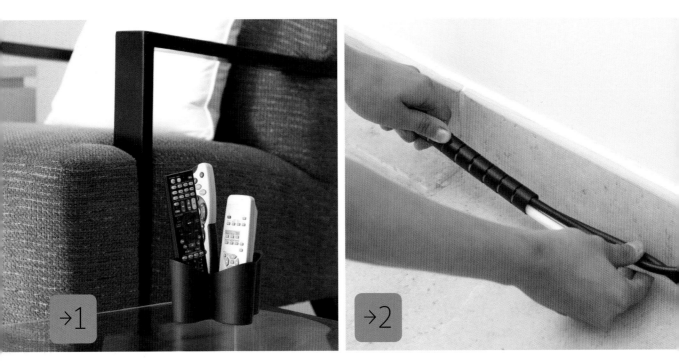

→1

→2

It's easy to waste time looking for the remote control when you need it. Stow it away in a remote-control caddy to help keep the room uncluttered.

Trailing cables can be hazardous. Either tuck them under the carpet or along the baseboard or, better still, gather them together in a cable organizer.

Extra tips

Declutter your equipment further by using wall-mounting kits where possible.

Declutter your music collection completely by transferring it all to your computer or MP3 player. But always keep a backup on an external hard drive.

Minimize the number of cables you have to plug into the power outlets by using an extension cord that incorporates several sockets. Make sure it's surge-protected to avoid damage to your electrical equipment in the event of a power surge. Some extension cords save energy by automatically switching off all the devices that are plugged in when the main device is switched off.

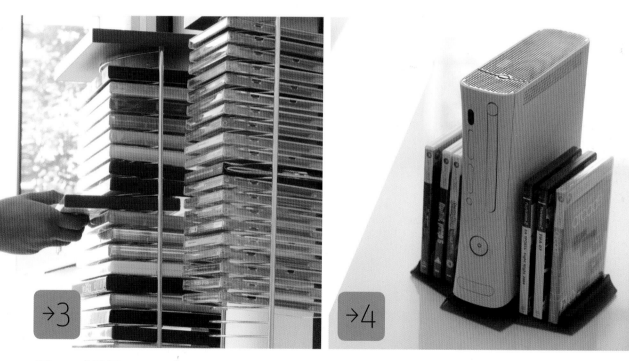

→3

→4

CDs and DVDs can take up a lot of space. Keep the room uncluttered and the discs dust-free by storing them in their boxes and stacking them in a storage unit.

Keep your games console and games neatly stored in a "gaming station." Get your family into the habit of putting these items away after use.

Pots and pans storage

An efficient kitchen will have everything on hand in the place where you need it. For ease of use, store frequently used pots, pans, and cooking implements near the stovetop and the oven. Saucepans and their lids take up a lot of room, but fortunately there are a number of storage devices on the market to choose from. Today's modern kitchens often have deep drawers and these can help solve your pan-storage problems.

PAN-LID HOLDER
Pan lids are notoriously difficult to store, but use one of these to provide a home for them. If you have enough cupboard space, put the pan-lid holder there.

BAKING EQUIPMENT STORAGE
Deep drawers are a pan-storage boon, especially now that many ovens don't have a storage drawer underneath. Reserve a deep drawer for your baking pans and trays.

STORAGE FOR LESS-USED ITEMS
Keep a low, deep drawer for pots and pans that you use less often.

PAN STANDS
Store bulky pans on a pan stand to free up cupboard space for other, less frequently used items.

HANGING RAIL AND HOOKS
Fix one of these on the wall close to your stove so your cooking implements will be close at hand. S-shaped hooks fit most handles.

Kitchen cupboard storage

Everyone's kitchen cupboards are different. Yours should contain the foods you use regularly, plus one or two items to keep in store in case you can't get to the grocery. To save wastage, don't overstock. Check the contents of your cupboard every month and bring items that are nearing their use-by date to the front so you use them in time and don't have to throw them away.

PRESERVING JARS
Use these for storing dry goods or homemade jams and preserves. Store open packages of dried goods in them, too. That way you can keep a check on the use-by date.

BOTTLED FOOD
Keep items you use regularly near the front, but check the use-by dates from time to time.

SPICE RACK
Keep only small quantities of herbs and spices, since they quickly lose their pungency. A revolving spice rack makes it easy to find the item you're looking for.

CANNED FOOD
This usually has a long shelf life but, as with bottled food, check the use-by dates regularly and bring the oldest items to the front. Never store half-used cans, since there's a risk of contamination. Instead, always decant and refrigerate in an airtight, covered container.

CRACKER CONTAINER
Store crackers and crispbreads in a moisture- and dust-proof container.

TALL CONTAINERS
Use tall glass containers to store spaghetti, fusilli lunghi, and any other long pasta shapes. The container keeps insects, dust, and moisture out, and you can see the contents at a glance.

CEREAL DISPENSER
Decant breakfast cereals into an airtight, moisture-proof dispenser to keep them dry and fresh for longer. A spout means you can pour the contents straight into your cereal bowl.

COOKIE JAR
Use a wide-bellied cookie jar to keep cookies dry. Cookies quickly absorb moisture from the air if left in an open package.

20 MIN Declutter a kitchen drawer

We all have a junk-filled drawer and it's often in the kitchen. The problem is that we waste precious time trying to find things. Declutter the drawer in minutes and you'll never lose that essential item again.

BARE ESSENTIALS

vacuum cleaner

crevice nozzle

sponge, plastic folders

ziplock bags, old envelopes

labels, drawer organizer

→1

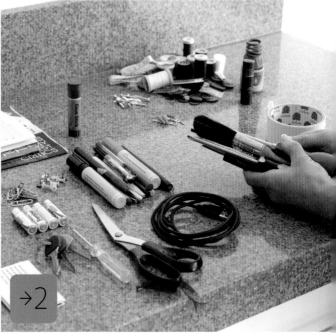

→2

Start by emptying everything out of the drawer. Vacuum inside with the crevice nozzle, then wipe the interior with a damp sponge to pick up any remaining debris.

Arrange the contents of the drawer, putting like with like so it's easy to see what's misplaced and needs to be put back correctly, and what to recycle or throw out.

Extra tips

When you return items to the decluttered drawer, put those you use often near the front and those you use less frequently toward the back.

While you're sorting the drawer, ask yourself the magic questions of decluttering (see p.193).

When you return something to a cluttered drawer, take a few minutes to declutter it there and then. If you really can't spare the time right away, be sure you return to do it within the week.

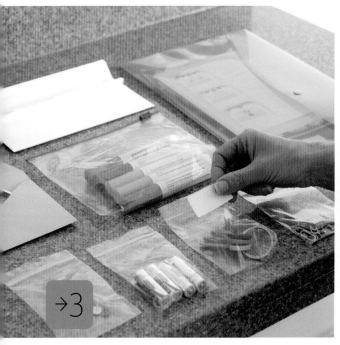

→3

Store instruction manuals in plastic folders with their receipts. Put flyers and business cards in old envelopes. Stow other items in plastic bags—labeled, if necessary.

→4

Replace the items whose home is the kitchen drawer. Don't overfill the drawer or you'll waste time looking for things. Use a drawer organizer if you wish.

Refrigerator storage

How and where you store food in your refrigerator, and how long you store it for are all important food-safety factors. Different areas of the refrigerator cool to slightly different temperatures, which is why it's important to store food in the correct area. Overall, the temperature inside your refrigerator should be 37.4°–41°F (3°–5°C). Bacteria multiply fast at higher temperatures. If you don't know how cool your refrigerator is, invest in a thermometer and adjust the temperature, if necessary. Finally, always wrap food correctly, and never keep it too long.

DAIRY PRODUCTS
Keep cheese and other dairy products well wrapped on the top shelf. Soft cheeses should keep for a week, hard cheeses for up to 3 weeks.

COOKED MEAT
Keep separate from raw meat. Store for 3–4 days in a glass dish covered with plastic wrap. Check the box to see if the plastic wrap is suitable for contact with the food. If it's not, stretch the plastic over the dish.

RAW MEAT AND POULTRY
Store for 3–5 days. Keep well wrapped in the lower part of the refrigerator to prevent blood from dripping. The blood may carry bacteria that can contaminate other food. Once meat is cooked, the risk of contamination falls.

FRESH VEGETABLES
Store these on the lower shelves for up to a week, depending on the type of vegetable. To prevent waste, check what you've got daily and use in soups and stir-fries before they wilt.

FRESH FRUIT
Some fruits will keep for 2 weeks in the fridge but, as with fresh vegetables, check regularly and use as quickly as possible.

MILK
Store milk in the refrigerator door to keep it within easy reach. It will keep from 1 to 2 weeks, depending on the fat content. Keep the container closed.

LEFTOVERS
Store leftovers in airtight lidded containers so they don't dry out. Try and eat within 2–4 days.

REFRIGERATOR DOOR
The temperature of the shelves in the door fluctuates more than in the main cabinet, so don't store highly perishable foods, such as fresh meat or fish, there. Don't open the door more than necessary and always close it as soon as possible.

LEMON FRESHENER
Sprinkle half a lemon with baking soda to keep the refrigerator smelling fresh. Replace as necessary, but at least every 2 weeks.

FRUIT DRINKS
Store these in the door or in the main compartment. Unopened cartons of fresh—non-heat-treated—juice will last up to 3 weeks, but you should use the contents of opened cartons in 7–10 days.

Freezer storage

Freezers are great for long-term food storage, but the bigger your freezer, the more chance you have of leaving food in it for too long. Yes, even frozen food can spoil! Check the contents of your freezer every few weeks so you don't forget to use what's in it or, better still, keep a magnetic notebook attached to the door with a list of what you put inside and when. Wrap food carefully to exclude as much air as possible and to keep food in peak condition, and if you're home-freezing, label everything with the date of freezing. But most important of all, you must keep your freezer at -4°F (-18°C) or below.

ICE PACKS
Have these accessible at the top of the freezer and use them for keeping picnic food cool or for keeping food cool while you clean the fridge.

UNFROZEN FOOD
When adding unfrozen items to the freezer, sandwich them between frozen ones so they freeze more quickly.

HOMEMADE MEALS
Store these in freezer-to-oven containers covered with aluminum foil, then you can take them out of the freezer and put them straight in the oven. Store for 4–6 months.

FISH PRODUCTS
Check recommended storage times on the packaging. Fresh fish storage times range from 4 months for oily fish to 10 months for flat fish.

UNCOOKED MEAT
Store on the bottom shelf to keep it from dripping on other items. Fresh meat can be stored for up to a year, depending on the type and cut.

ICE POPS
Keep these on a shallow shelf, then they'll be easier to find.

ICE CUBES
Store on the top shelf so food doesn't leak onto them.

ICE CREAM
Keep this accessible and near the top. Store-bought ice cream should keep for 6 months.

FROZEN FRUIT AND VEGETABLES
If home-frozen, keep in labeled freezer bags fastened with clips or wire ties and marked with the date of freezing. Home-frozen fruit keeps for 8 months to a year and home-frozen vegetables for up to a year. Commercially frozen fruit keeps for a year and vegetables for 12–18 months.

BREAD PRODUCTS
Store these all together for up to 3 months.

LEFTOVER FOOD
Store this, together with homemade soups and fruit purées, in freezer-proof lidded containers. Label with the date and contents. Store food that includes cooked meat or poultry for 2–6 months.

INDIVIDUAL PORTIONS
Divide items such as sausages into single portions and store in sealed, labeled plastic bags. It's hard to separate individual items when they're frozen together. Store bacon and sausages for 1–2 months.

FROZEN POULTRY
Store chicken or turkey for a maximum of a year.

10 TIPS Decluttering the hall

All too often, the hallway becomes a dumping ground for things you're in too much of a rush to sort out when you arrive home. Prevent hallway chaos and keep your hall organized and clutter-free by following these easy tips.

1 STORE IN A CLOSET
Your first line of attack for a clutter-free hall is providing somewhere to stow coats, jackets, hats, scarves, and bags. A hall closet is the neatest solution. Failing that, use wall-mounted hooks.

2 BE NEAT
Encourage the family to hang up their outdoor clothes as soon as they come into the house, unless the clothes are wet, in which case, see tip 3. And encourage them not to dump things in the hall as they pass.

3 DRY OFF WET CLOTHES
Never put damp clothes away in a closet or they'll get musty and mildewed. Attach an over-the-door hook to the hall closet door or to another door and hang wet outdoor clothing there.

4 KEEP UP WITH THE SEASONS
Don't waste precious space by keeping out-of-season outdoor clothing in the hall. Instead, sort through what you've got every spring and fall, and store the things you don't need (see pp.210 and 213).

5 BE SELECTIVE

Don't use the hallway as the place to store all the family's accessories. Select the bags, scarves, and hats you use regularly and put the rest in drawers and closets elsewhere in the home.

6 USE A SHOE RACK

If you have a "shoes-off" rule in your house, place a shoe rack in the hallway to keep shoes neat and tidy. You may be able to fit a shoe rack in the hall closet if you have one, which will be even neater.

7 PICK UP THE MAIL

If mail is delivered through a door letter slot and lands on the hall floor, don't leave it there to add to the clutter. Pick it up right away and put letters in a tray to deal with later. Recycle junk mail and unwanted flyers.

8 STORE KEYS SAFELY

Don't leave keys on a hall table or hanging from a hook in the hallway. A burglar might be able to access them through a window or letter slot in the front door. Fix key hooks or a secure key box on the kitchen wall.

9 CLEAR THE GARBAGE

Don't keep garbage bags in the hallway waiting to be taken outside. They smell, may leak on the floor, and add to the clutter. Instead, take out the garbage as soon as the bags are full.

10 USE A BASKET

Have a basket at the bottom of the stairs to collect things that have to be taken up. This keeps the hallway clutter-free, but make sure you keep the basket somewhere where you won't trip over it.

20 MIN Declutter a closet

At least once a year, sort through the contents of your wardrobe. It only takes a few minutes and you'll be left with a beautifully decluttered closet where you can find just what you need in a moment.

BARE ESSENTIALS

under-bed storage boxes and/or moisture- and dust-proof clothes storage bags

selection of clothes hangers

→1 **Arrange the contents** of your closet in piles. One pile is to give to charity, one is for washing or dry-cleaning, and one is for keeping.

→2 **Now sort through the pile** of clothes you are keeping. Pack unseasonal clothes away in under-bed storage boxes or in moisture- and dust-proof storage bags.

Extra tips

Be ruthless. If you haven't worn something for over two years, it's time to give it to a friend or pass it on to the thrift store.

Don't hang heavy knitwear or long knitted dresses on hangers or they'll lose their shape. Instead, fold them and store them in a drawer or on a shelf.

As you declutter your clothing, check for moth damage. If there is any and it's not too bad, have the clothing dry-cleaned. This will kill any moths and larvae. Throw out damaged clothing and, to prevent future problems, use moth repellant (see p.213) and check the closet every few weeks.

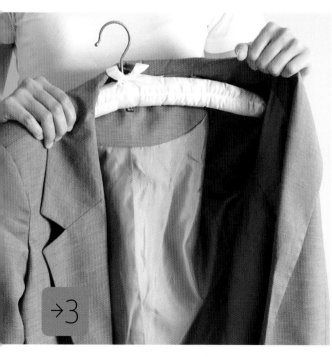

→3

Place clothes on hangers. Don't ruin the shape of clothes by using wire hangers. Use wooden, plastic, or padded hangers, and clip hangers for pants and skirts.

→4

As you replace items in the closet, keep like with like to help you find items quickly. Group jackets, pants, suits, skirts, dresses, blouses, and shirts.

Caring for clothes and shoes

10 TIPS

The secret to keeping clothes in tip-top condition is having clean, well-organized storage space and never putting dirty clothes away. Moths are your number one enemy, but follow these simple tips, and your clothes will last for years.

1 CLEAN OUT DRAWERS AND CLOSETS
A couple of times a year, empty all drawers and closets, vacuum thoroughly, wash, rinse, and leave to dry. Line shelves and drawers with lining paper. This all helps to deter moths.

✔

2 KEEP MOTHS AT BAY
Check clothing twice a year for signs of moth damage. Either dispose of damaged clothing or have it dry-cleaned to kill the larvae. Deter moths with lavender sachets and cedarwood blocks in drawers and closets.

✔

3 ALTERNATE YOUR CLOTHING
Avoid wearing the same clothes or shoes on two consecutive days. Clothes last longer and look fresher if they have a chance to air. Hang clothes up while still warm from the body and the creases will drop out.

✔

4 KEEP CLOTHES IN SHAPE
When hanging up clothes, fasten the top, middle, and bottom buttons, close the zippers, and empty all the pockets. Don't overfill your closet—clothes need space or they'll get musty—and don't hang heavy knitwear.

✔

5 AVOID UNNECESSARY WASHING
Washing clothes too often can cause them to fade and fray. If you've only worn an item briefly and it's not dirty, hang it to air overnight in a well-ventilated place before putting it away.

6 STORE UNSEASONAL CLOTHES
Sort through your clothes every spring and fall. Wash or dry-clean unseasonal clothing—moths like dirty clothes—repair if necessary, then store in dustproof bags, boxes, suitcases, or trunks.

7 GROUP UNDERWEAR
Use separate drawers for bras, underwear, and socks, or use a drawer organizer to create separate compartments in one drawer. Store bras with one cup inside the other so they keep their shape.

8 KEEP SHOES IN PAIRS
Store shoes in pairs on a shoe rack, in a canvas hanging organizer, or in labeled boxes or boxes with a clear window so you can see which pair is inside.

9 DRY WET SHOES THOROUGHLY
If shoes are very wet, pack them with newspaper or paper towels and leave them to dry naturally before putting them away. This will prevent them from losing their shape.

10 PREVENT SHOE SMELLS
Sprinkle the inside of smelly shoes with baking soda and let them air overnight. The next morning, shake or vacuum the powder out.

Home office storage

You'll work more efficiently in your home office when everything you need is neat and close at hand. Gather up all your clutter by using storage trays, desk caddies, and filing systems, but choose items that suit your specific needs, or you'll simply end up with a clutter of storage solutions. And no matter how long you spend at your desk, invest in a good chair. It's better for your back—and when your back's comfortable, your mind will be clearer.

DESK CHAIR
Make sure your desk chair is comfortable. At a minimum it should provide good lumbar—lower-back—support, must be height-adjustable, and have lockable castors. Ideally, it should also support the sacrum—the bone at the base of the spine—and the depth of the seat and the arms should all be adjustable.

FILING TRAYS
Stackable trays save space on your desk. Use to hold papers that you need as you work, as well as papers that are waiting to be filed away.

DESK CADDY
Choose one with a number of different-sized compartments to hold pens, pencils, paperclips, rubber bands, and all the other small office paraphernalia you need.

HOME FILE
Buy one that contains hanging files and use it for storing papers that you only need occasionally. If you're short of shelf space, keep it on the floor, but not where you might trip over it.

DOCUMENT WALLETS
Use these to keep papers together for the projects that you're currently working on.

STICKY NOTES
Have a variety of sizes and colors for different purposes.

MAGAZINE FILE
Store magazines and brochures here and, if you're short of space, sort them regularly and throw away any you no longer need.

WASTE-PAPER BASKET
Essential for helping to keep your home office neat. If you have room, you could have two baskets—one for recyclable material.

10 TIPS

Declutter an attic or basement

An attic or basement may seem to offer the ultimate storage solution, but if you don't plan your storage properly, these rooms can soon lapse into chaos. Follow these simple, methodical tips for clutter-free storage that works.

1 CULL UNWANTED ITEMS
Before you begin, take a long, hard look at what you have. Do you really need it? Have you used it in the last year? Have you missed it? If any of your answers are "no," then donate the item, sell it, or throw it out. ✔

2 START TO SEPARATE
Now assess what you have left to store, and everything else will follow. Separate what's seasonal from what needs short- or long-term storage, then plan what containers you'll need and in which sizes. ✔

3 CONSIDER ACCESS AND LIGHT
Review your storage space and plan to put the things you need to access most often nearest the door. Make sure, too, that the room's well lit so when you need something, you don't have to grope in the dark to find it. ✔

4 GET THE RIGHT STORAGE
Choose storage that does the job. Make sure it fits the things you're keeping and that it's dust- and damp-proof. Stackable storage will help to save space. ✔

5 LABEL, LABEL, LABEL

The only way to find things quickly is to label them, and in general, the bigger the labels, the better. What's more, when a thing's labeled, you can send someone else to find it.

6 USE THE WALLS

Make the most of the wall space by putting up hooks and attaching plenty of shelving. This not only helps keep the floor clear, but also gives you somewhere to store smaller items.

7 KEEP A PATH CLEAR

There's no point in storing stuff if you can't get to it. Make sure you leave a clear path through the boxes and don't fill the entire floor space.

8 LEAVE SPACE IN CONTAINERS

Chances are there are stairs to your attic or basement, in which case, don't overfill your storage containers and make them too heavy. When you need to get them out, you don't want to risk injury.

9 KEEP A NOTE

Keep a note of everything you've stored away and where exactly you've put it. Months and occasionally years might pass before you need a particular item and it may be very hard to remember where it is.

10 KEEP IT CLEAN

There's nothing worse than having to deal with dusty, cobwebby boxes. Once a year, take everything out of storage, dust the containers, and vacuum or sweep the floor.

10 TIPS Running a thrifty household

It's wise not to waste your money—or the Earth's resources. These thrifty tips cover everything from budgeting to food and from cleaning to clothes care. Follow these pain-free suggestions and you'll be well on the way to running a truly thrifty household.

1 SAVE ENERGY
Turn lights off when you leave a room; keep thermostats low and wear an extra layer; reduce your water usage; buy energy-efficient electrical goods—all these will save you money and help save the planet.

✓

2 HAVE A BUDGET
There are good budget planners online that will show you how much you spend each year and what you spend it on. If you're spending more than you earn, the planner will help you see where to cut back.

✓

3 BE A SMART SHOPPER
Always arm yourself with a shopping list, don't shop for food when you're hungry, and only shop once a week. These are tried-and-tested tips that will save you from temptation.

✓

4 BUY CHEAP
When you're shopping for everyday items, buy the cheapest product that does the job effectively. Save by buying in bulk and if you can bear it, cut out meat and watch your food bills plummet.

✓

5 KEEP THE FREEZER FULL

A full freezer uses less electricity than a half-full one, so save money by keeping your freezer as packed as possible. If there are large gaps, fill them with old milk cartons filled with water.

6 GROW YOUR OWN

There's a burgeoning interest in growing your own food. Try it out, even if it's just a few herbs on the patio, some windowsill greens, or a mini fruit tree or tomatoes in a pot.

7 LEARN TO SEW

All you need to know is the basics. Learn how to sew on a button or stitch up a hem. You'll prolong the life of your clothes and save money that you'd otherwise spend on repairs.

8 USE UP PRODUCTS COMPLETELY

To use the last drop of a cleaning product, add a splash of water to the bottle, and to reach the last squeeze of creams and pastes, cut the containers open to reveal what's left inside.

9 GIVE NEW LIFE TO OLD

Use old toothbrushes for scrubbing in hard-to-reach corners and for cleaning grouting; cut up old T-shirts to use as dust cloths; and use old ice-cream tubs and other lidded food containers for food storage.

10 USE THIS BOOK

The tips in this book will save you money. Keep your home and clothing clean and things will last longer and need to be replaced less often. Use natural cleaning products and save money on your weekly grocery bill.

Index

Acknowledgments

Dorling Kindersley would like to thank Tamsin Weston for
props styling, Gary Kemp for retouching, Adam Brackenbury
for the symbols artwork, Tessa Bindloss for design assistance,
Danaya Bunnag for modeling and for helping out, Roxanne
Benson-Mackey for modeling, Emma Sergeant, Ria Osborne,
and Liz Franks for assisting the photographer and for modeling,
Hers Agency Ltd. for providing the props stylist, j-me product
designs for supplying props, 1st Option for the location house.